PALMISTRY
MADE EASY
Fred Gettings

Published by
Melvin Powers
WILSHIRE BOOK COMPANY
12015 Sherman Road
No. Hollywood, California 91605
Telephone: (213) 875-1711

First published 1966 by
Bancroft & Co. (Publishers) Ltd.,
Greencoat House,
Francis Street, London, S. W. 1.
Copyright 1966 by
Bancroft & Co. Ltd.,
All rights reserved

Printed by

HAL LEIGHTON PRINTING COMPANY
P.O. Box 3952
North Hollywood, California 91605
Telephone: (213) 983-1105

Printed in the United States of America

ISBN 0-87980-114-X

Contents

The publishers wish to acknowledge the kind permission given by HONEY magazine to use the material at pages 138 to 145

4

1

The following prints are reproduced by kind permission of the PALMISTRY magazine to the chapter of pages 170 to 174

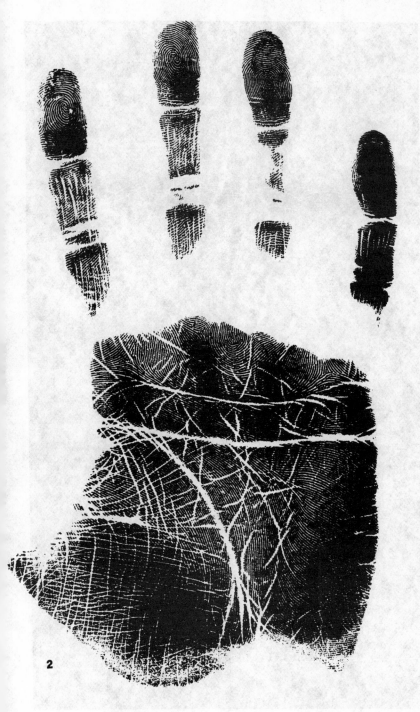

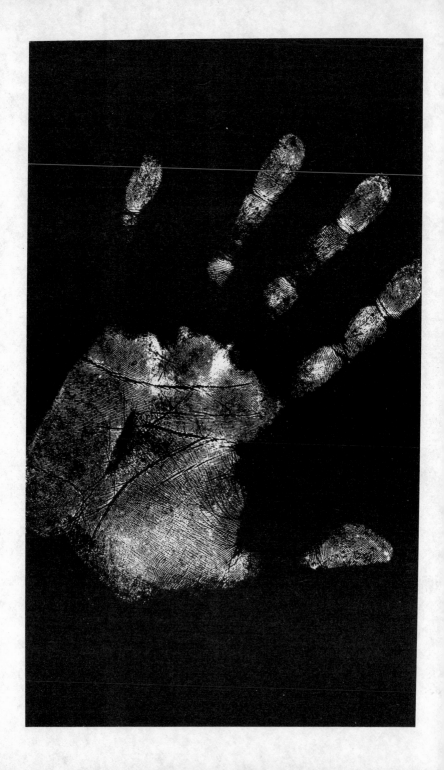

Preface

PALMISTRY is a fascinating subject. It is one of the oldest of the ancient 'occult' sciences, and is even mentioned in the earliest known Indian writings; yet in spite of this, it is a study very relevant to modern life. In palmistry many subjects meet — medicine, psychology, morphology, astrology, endocrinology and many more — yet it remains essentially a simple study, based on the assumption that it is possible to judge by appearance. Palmistry can be studied on many levels. You can learn something of the simple basic theory and put this into use in your daily contact with people, for example, in helping you form judgements of character; or you can devote much of your time to the subject, read and study widely and eventually construct your own special system and begin an adventure with new ideas.

This book is designed to start the beginner off on either of these roads. The basic theory of hand types and certain teachings concerning the meaning of the lines are presented in a simple and, I hope, interesting manner. With the information contained in the following pages you will find both a basic framework for more prolonged study or sufficient background knowledge to entertain yourself and your friends with accounts of their personality and character traits.

I hope that this book will achieve its aim of introducing the reader to something of the real pleasure and excitement I have experienced in my own study of this intriguing subject. Whether the approach is made in a spirit of objective scientific enquiry, or in a spirit of fun, it is certain that you will find much enjoyment and pleasure — and a great deal to surprise you!

3

1 *Female school teacher*
2 *Male office manager*
3 *Fourteen month old daughter of the couple in the two plates opposite. The example shows quite clearly that the old belief that the hand of the child resembles the hand of one or other of the parents is just so much nonsense. The short fingers are more like those of the father (plate 2), whilst the downward sweep of the line of head is more like that of the mother. The finger print patterns, however, resemble neither parent — as can be seen from the pattern on the index finger, there is a basic loop pattern, whereas both the index fingers of the parents bear a whorl pattern of almost concentric circles. The clear lines under the ring finger indicates that provided the education of the child is properly balanced she will be a much more creative person than either of her parents, for she will find it easier to give material expression to her emotions. The short index finger suggests that she will manifest the same social attitudes as her father, which springs from a sense of inadequacy.*

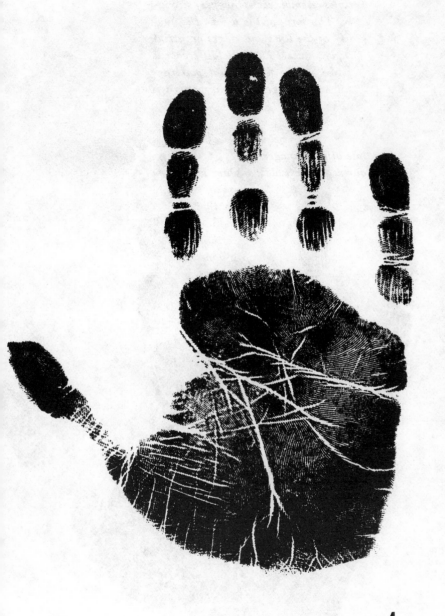

4 *Right and left prints of a ten year*
5 *old boy, showing how hands some-*
times resemble each other very strong-
ly. The form of the hands, the qua-
lity of the lines and ridges are strik-
ingly similar. The basic difference is
found in the finger print patterns—
finger for finger, not one pattern is
alike.

5

What is Palmistry? Some basic facts

Few people are more inclined to criticize palmistry than those who know nothing about it. Frequently, when I am introduced to people as having made a close study of palmistry, I meet the bland question, "But surely you don't believe in things like that?". Usually no answer to the question is required, and they will go on to explain how the crease lines (which to them are the only concern of palmistry) are the result of flexion and can bear no relation whatsoever to the future. It is useless to attempt to explain that 'crease' lines, the future, destiny and fate are merely the outward trappings of a kind of palmistry long out of date, and that the word palmistry also refers to something quite outside the usual connotation. It is not a question of belief — palmistry exists. The choice is only whether to accept or reject it; and only ignorance can reject as worthless something which it has not investigated.

The principle behind palmistry is extremely simple and we employ it consciously or unconsciously every day of our life. It is natural for us to judge by appearance — to assume that if a man laughs he is happy, if he turns pale he is either ill or frightened, if he wrinkles his brow he is thinking. We judge the inner state from the outer manifestation, and it is no more remarkable (and for that matter no less miraculous) that we should be able to tell something about a person from his hand than that we should be able to tell something about him from his face.

If a person laughs we assume he is amused. We may, of course, be wrong, but more often than not we are right — for our general experience has led us to connect laughter, which is an outward thing, with amusement, which is an inner thing. Similarly, if a person has a long nail phalange on his little finger (plate 30), we can assure that he will have considerable linguistic ability. Again, we may be wrong in the individual case — but general experience shows that on the whole it is correct to connect the two.

Palmistry, like medicine, like Science itself, is a pragmatic thing — the result of an attempt on the part of Mankind to create order out of chaos, to find meaning and significance in an outward form — and because of this mistakes can be made. Palmistry, like all other forms of knowledge, consists of a series of hypotheses — and it is only right that these should be open to criticism. It is unfortunate for palmistry and for the more honest palmists that charlatans have justified much of the criticism which has been levelled at them, and it is of paramount importance to realise that there is palmistry and 'palmistry', palmists and 'palmists'. The majority of people who condemn this ancient study either know nothing about it (and therefore condemn only themselves) or have met only one variety of palmistry, know only one kind of palmist, and condemn only these.

The best known form of palmistry is, of course, the palmistry of the seaside piers, garden fêtes and subdued drawing rooms, and of this I can say little. I have only on one or two occasions been impressed by what I have seen of this kind of palmistry, and I know that on the whole it is a waste of time and money.

Some years ago I stood on a seaside pier and watched a long queue of men and women (mainly

6

women) pay their money, thrust in turn their hands through a narrow hole, and have their hands 'read'. Approximately three minutes — never more than four — were sufficient for the 'palmist' to determine and say what was required of them. My reaction to this ritual led me to think a great deal about the nature of palmistry — of *that* kind of palmistry — and it soon became clear that it catered for people seeking reassurance, security and certainty, in a world where such qualities do not exist.

As a direct result of this conclusion, I determined that I would only practise and study palmistry in future in the interests of what I could learn, suppressing any urge to entertain, impress or mystify the people who let me see their hands.

It was only at this stage that my real study of palmistry began. Part of my reaction on the pier. sprang from my knowledge that the palmists could not be learning or saying anything of value in the time they allowed themselves. Their speed astonished and upset me, for I knew that at least two hours of careful study are required to make even the most tentative of conclusions when using the traditional forms of palmistry. No doubt these traditional forms are quite beyond the grasp of these 'palmists' on the pier.

But what is *real* palmistry? I am not sure that a complete answer can be given. Palmistry is essentially a search for truth, and its final form will depend on the one who seeks. Perhaps a more simple answer can be given if we understand that there are two different kinds of real palmistry, and both can be studied and practised either separately or together. One is the palmistry of the intellect, and

6 Right and left prints of a female
7 shorthand typist.

In contrast to the previous pair of prints, these two show marked contrasts. Although the two hands have the same general characteristics, there are great variations in the lines—for example, the right hand has a much more clearly defined (though broken) girdle of Venus above the line of Heart, whilst the left hand contains a clear line of Mercury. There is, however, a much closer resemblence in the finger patterns—though the left ring finger has a loop pattern, and the right ring finger has a whorl pattern. It is interesting to compare this richly lined hand with the one at plates 4 and 5—it is characteristic of a type more neurotic and less harmonious than the young boy. It is a typically feminine hand, whilst the earlier one is a typical masculine hand.

the other is the palmistry of the emotions.

The palmistry of the intellect is the kind of palmistry which, by tradition, relates a long nail phalange with linguistic ability. It is the sort of palmistry which is linked to our tendency to judge by appearances, to assume that if a man laughs he must be happy.

The other kind of palmistry – the palmistry of the emotions – is less familiar and more difficult to

7

define. We all know that we can come to quite definite conclusions about people without knowing precisely how or why we come to these conclusions — that we can, for instance, suspect that although a man is laughing, he may be only trying to give the impression that he is amused. It is in this same sense that intuitive judgements may be made from the hand. Intuitive judgements are a part and parcel of our everyday experience, and it is only natural that such judgements should play an important part in palmistry. As you become more and more familiar with the outward features of different hands, you will become gradually aware of qualities *behind* the appearance.

Both these types of palmistry can be best illustrated by two short anecdotes.

Some months ago I was commissioned to do character analyses of certain celebrities, and this involved visiting them in their homes or at their work. On one such visit I found myself with an hour or so spare during a live performance in a London television studio. There was the usual clamour from other people in the studio for me to 'read their hands', and as there is usually a wide variety of interesting types in such places I made a number of hand prints whilst waiting for the actor to finish. My practice in such circumstances is to take prints on sheets of paper and to ask the people to write their names, addresses and occupations on the sheets in case I should wish to find more about their life, temperament or background.

When I reached home later that day I looked through the collection of prints and was very much impressed by a hand print which was quite different from anything I had seen before (plate 8). Although there was a name on the sheet, there was no address and no occupation. The name meant nothing to me, so I did a fairly brief analysis to work out what sort of person this could be. A few days later I was having a drink with my agent and I brought up the subject of this impressive hand, asking if he knew anything about the person. He laughed when I told him the name on the sheet, and asked me what sort of person I thought the subject would be from his print. I said that he was obviously a very special person — quite refined, something of a law unto himself, very interested in physical exercise and clearly possessed of a strong physique. The form of the hand, with such interesting papillary ridge patterns on the finger tips made it difficult to categorize him — he would certainly be a versatile extremist of some kind. Once more my agent laughed. "I 'm not surprised — though very impressed — by what you say: that is the hand of Mr. Universe!"

The story serves to illustrate the intellectual form of palmistry — the drawing up of a character by comparing specific hand qualities such as lines, ridge formations, size of fingers and shape of palm, and relating these to create a simple pattern of

8 The hand of "Mr. Universe 1965". Powerful hand traits, such as the strong lines, massive palm (in spite of its size, not square in shape) and the whorl patterns on the middle and index fingers indicate a forceful personality and excellent physique.

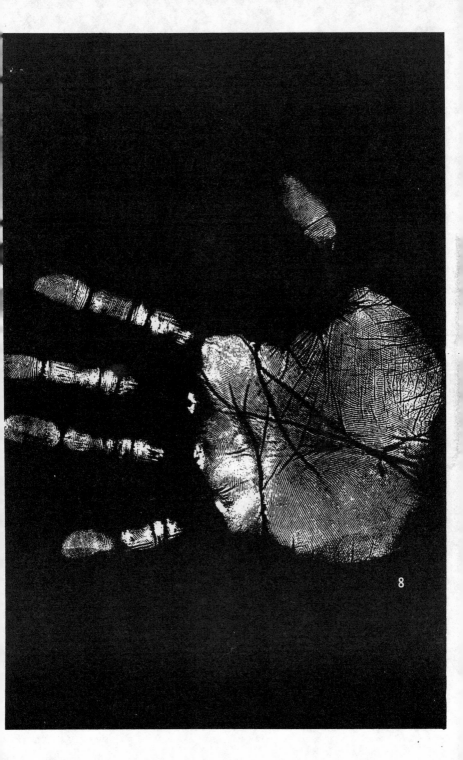

8

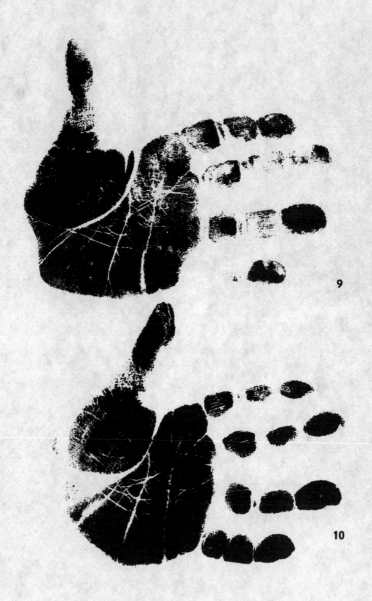

> 9 *Fourteen month old girl. Two more*
> 10 *prints made at the same time as the*
> *one reproduced at plate 3 indicate*
> *some of the dangers of palmistry.*
> *Neither print is very good from the*
> *point of view of itellectual palm-*
> *istry; in plate 9 the ball of the*
> *thumb is pressed into the palm, and*
> *gives the hand a much more narrow*
> *appearance than it has in plate 10.*
> *The lines on plate 10 have none of*
> *the clarity of those on plate 9. The*
> *lines between the Life line and the*
> *Head line are of considerable im-*
> *portance in this case, as they were*
> *changing fairly quickly, as can be*
> *seen from the print at plate 11.*

behaviour. It is palmistry in which the analytic quality of the brain is brought into play. There is no
great mystery to this form of palmistry — it is an intellectual exercise which can be learned as one learns
a language. It is a palmistry which depends on a
certain knowledge, and an ability to marshal facts
into a pattern.

My second anecdote is shorter and illustrates
quite a different kind of palmistry. I was in a
friend's flat one evening discussing various things
including palmistry. She asked me if I would look
at her hand to tell her whether or not she was going
to marry the man with whom she was currently in
love. I didn't commit myself to telling her anything, but I did undertake to examine her hand.
Almost as soon as I saw it I said, "What does the

name Eric mean to you?" She looked at me in asto-
nishment and exclaimed, "But that's his name..."
I told her that she had to be very careful with Eric,
and advised her to find out a little more about him. I
would say no more, passing the conversation on to
other topics, as I knew that Eric was already married!
A few days later she rang me to say that she had been
upset to find that her boyfriend already had a wife!

Now, it is quite impossible for me to explain *how*
I knew Eric's name and matrimonial state — quite
certainly it is quite impossible to arrive at either by
means of the intellectual kind of palmistry. Such
knowledge belongs to an entirely different order of
things within us. It is an intuitive knowledge—information derived from unknown sources by the emó-
tions, which are somehow more sensitive and perceptive than our rather cumbersome intellect. It is
almost as if a part of us (with which our emotions
may sometimes be in contact) knows everything
about the past, present and future, and participates
only very rarely in our conscious life. The kind of
palmistry which the story illustrates, and which
springs from this inner store of wisdom, is called
'intuitive' palmistry.

It almost goes without saying that this sort of
judgement could be arrived at without necessarily
looking at the subject's hands. His or her posture,
facial expression and vocal intonation would perhaps form a satisfactory springboard for such an
emotional judgement. The secret is, however, to become keenly aware of the hand, with its complex of
highly sensitive nerves, and its significant outer
form, and to become so familiar with it, both
emotionally and intellectually, that your judge-

11 *The same hand eight months later. The delicate tracery of lines between the lines of Life and Head have developed considerably. Although the three prints reproduced on these two pages would cause a great deal of trouble for an intellectual palmist, a really good "intuitive" palmist would be able to arrive at more or less the same conclusions from any of the three prints. Of course, children's prints are difficult to make, though they more easily show variations in line strengths and directions, as the crease lines tend to charge considerably during infancy. The four prints of this child indicate how the method of making prints is invaluable for recording the linear qualities of a hand, but rather dubious (especially with soft or flexible hands, like the one illustrated) for recording the form of the hand.*

11

12 Four and a half year old girl. This hand must be compared with the one at plate 13, which is a print of her sister's hand. The prints are different in form and line. The fingers on plate 12 are a little shorter, and the palm is more square in form. There is a richer pattern of crease lines. These palmistic differences suggest that in temperament the younger girl will be more harmoniously adapted to life, and will have a richer inner world of imagination. She will be quieter, less "outgoing" and not so egocentric as her sister.

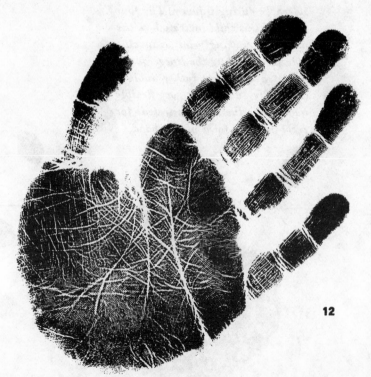

12

ments will be made quickly and certainly. After some practice you will find it difficult to determine exactly where your use of intellectual palmistry ends and the use of emotional palmistry begins — and it is at this point that you will be practising palmistry in its deepest sense.

Both forms of palmistry must be studied. The practice and study of the intellectual form is, of course, simply a matter of application, and this guide will be especially useful in this respect, for it sets out the fundamental rules which govern thought judgements. The 'intuitive' kind of palmistry is not entirely passed over, however, even though this is much more a matter of individual experimentation and inner effort. The few notes on page 50 may help you in this direction.

Palmistry has been defined as 'The art of telling character or fortune from the lines and markings on the hand.' This is a 'popular' definition and is not very exact, for the art proper is concerned with more than the lines and markings on the hand surface, and in fact takes the entire hand as its subject.

The haphazard manner in which palmistry has evolved through the ages has resulted in two branches of study which are sometimes integrated into one system (as with my own system, outlined in this book), sometimes developed separately. This is sometimes completely misunderstood. The two branches of palmistry are Chiromancy and Chirognomy.

Chiromancy has an unhappy connotation nowadays. It may be equated with the earlier forms of palmistry which were concerned chiefly with the study of the lines on the palmar surface. When one talks about Chiromancy one is in fact referring to a somewhat out-of-date system of fixed symbol interpretations which has survived, with surprisingly little change, for many centuries. Because of its obvious connection with ancient methods, with charlatans, gypsies and popular articles in women's magazines, chiromancy is usually thought of as dealing with the past and future of the subject.

Chirognomy was not developed to any great extent until the last century. Since that time there has been an undue emphasis on this branch of the study, to such an extent, indeed, that the more advanced books on palmistry tend to dismiss almost entirely the chiromantical side in favour of chirognomy. The word chirognomy refers to the study of the form of the hand – to the fingers, palm, nails and so on.

Real palmistry consists of a balance of judgements relating both Chiromancy and Chirognomy into one study. Although each of the two branches must be studied separately, they must be constantly inter-related if valid judgements are to be made concerning the subject.

The ancient belief, which persists to a great extent today, that the form of the hand relates to the character of the person, whilst the lines on the hand leave a clue to the past and future, is just so much nonsense. Only a little reflection is required to see the absurdity of thinking that a man's destiny, fate or chance life happenings are somehow separate from his character. A man doesn't make his own life and control consciously his mode of living – he reacts to the external stimuli of life in terms of his own character. To a very large extent the pattern of a person's life is determined by a combination of three

13 *Six year old girl. The richer patterns on the finger ends (especially on the index and ring fingers) suggest a more extraverted personality with a more volatile temperament. Slightly longer palm and longer fingers indicate that she will be a little more unstable than her sister.*

13

14 *This print is the left hand of one of the sisters at plates 12 and 13. The fact that it is not at first apparent which hand it accompanies indicates just how much variation in form and line there can be between the left and right hand of one person. It is almost impossible to determine*

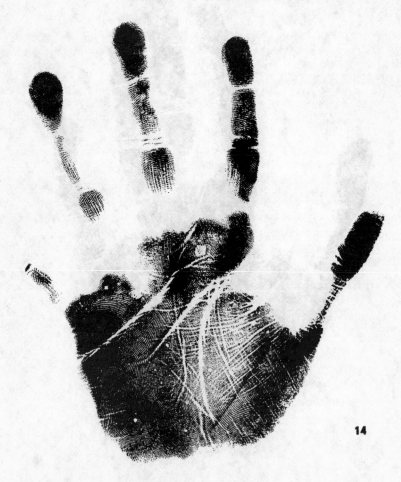

14

forces – disposition of character, subconscious aim and pure chance. Real palmistry (that is intellectual and intuitive palmistry combined) can investigate and pronounce on each of these three forces. It cannot pronounce with any certainty on the chance happenings – though these are limited in a curious way by other factors which may be determined – so an absolute prediction of future events is never possible. One can indicate only directions and tendencies.

As I say, the study of real palmistry involves the combination of judgements made from a chiromantical standpoint and judgements made from a chirognomical standpoint. In the early stages it will be found that chiromancy can best be studied from prints made directly from the hand, whilst chirognomy can best be studied from good photographs of the hand. The several hours required for a detailed study of one hand renders it very unlikely that a subject will be inclined to hold out his hand for direct examination. The method of print making is described on page 32. Photographs are difficult to take: although I often use a Rollei for record purposes, I find that a professional photographer is the best source of good photographs for detailed study and for reproduction in articles and books. The many books on palmistry – especially the good ones by such people as Benham, Spier, Mangoldt and Muchèry – contain interesting prints which may be studied at leisure. It is essential that once you are satisfied that palmistry will be a source of lasting interest you build up a collection of prints and photographs for reference purposes. A library of books on the subject will also be very

which person the print belongs to from the form of the hand, which is distorted by the typically extravert open fingers. The clue is found in the rich finger patterns, and the relative lack of lines around the middle of the palm.

15 Male cartoonist on a British Daily Newspaper.

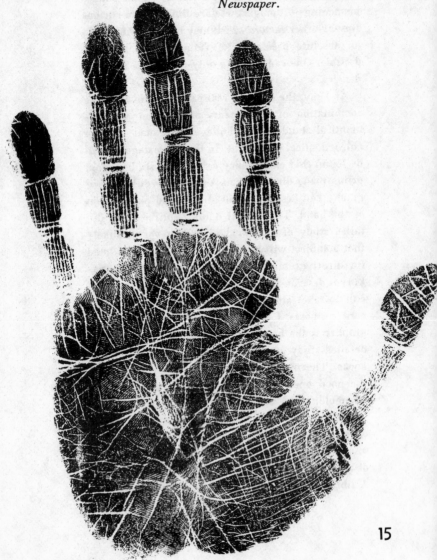

15

useful. I append a list of the most satisfactory books on palmistry which will be invaluable for further reading and for following up the ideas outlined in this book. The allied subjects of astrology, alchemy, magic and even general philosophy contribute a great deal to palmistry and the more cosmopolitan one's reading the more profound will be one's judgements. It is worth mentioning that it is illegal to practice palmistry. Most people are genuinely surprised at this — and they are even more surprised to learn that even to advertise as a palmist (or astrologer, for that matter) is illegal. On the whole, however, very few prosecutions are brought against the practitioners of the various occult studies, and it is rather to be considered a good thing that subjects with so much potential danger from a psychological point of view should be at least nominally illegal.

I shall deal with a few of the dangers inherent in the practice of palmistry, and make a few notes about the spirit in which the study should be conducted a little later on. For the moment all I can say is that I hope that this simple guide will introduce you to the sort of undertaking and study in which I have delighted over the past few years. I hope that you will find palmistry as fascinating and rewarding as I have done, and that you will benefit from making this study. If I may conclude this preface with a word of advice. I would say that it is imperative that you should not forget your original aim — you are studying palmistry to learn — not to show off your 'occult powers'. On the whole the practice of palmistry has not got a good name — try at least not to make the name any worse!

Introductory Notes on the Hand

PERHAPS the easiest way to come to grips with the problems involved in the study of palmistry is to begin by looking carefully at your own hand. A complete analysis of your own hand, as indeed of any other hand, involves both a chirognomical and chiromantical study, and it is therefore necessary to examine the live hand as well as carefully prepared prints, which are vital to the study of the linear formations on the hand surface. Your first task, therefore, will be to prepare one or two prints of each of your hands to help you in your examination.

The materials required for print making are very simple — paper, padding, ink and a roller. The paper surface must be fairly smooth — I find a smooth typewriting paper ideal for the purpose, as the quarto sheet is large enough to take most hands, and the weight of the paper is quite suitable. The sheet of paper upon which you intend to make your impression must be placed either on a firm wad of paper sheets or on a flat rubber base, such as those used under typewriters to deaden the noise of the keys. Should you use a wad of paper, it should be about threequarters of an inch in thickness to allow a cushion which will give' to the surface of the printing sheet in order to permit it to mould slightly to the uneven form of the hand.

Almost any kind of printing ink will suffice for making hand prints — though a water based ink facilitates the cleaning of the hand after an impression has been made. A water-based lino printing ink is very suitable. The roller, of the kind used for lino printing, should be of a fair width — six inches is the ideal, for with such a roller you can make a

16 *A bad print from the hand of an eighteen year old Spanish girl. This print is reproduced to show what effects must be avoided in print making. The typically peasant palm, which is masculine in appearance, was heavy and hard, and would not meet the flat surface of the paper and the central hollow resulted. In addition certain lines, particularly those to the right of the hollow, were distorted under the pressure. The roots of the two middle fingers are not printed clearly enough. These three undesireable effets can be rectified by rubbing the paper on to the inked hand.*

17 *Eighteen month old girl. Sometimes it is very difficult to obtain a clear print of the fingers, as in this example, and the only thing one can do is to make a note of their length relative to the palm, their individual lengths and the finger patterns. A photograph is quite useful in these circumstances.*

direct inking along the whole width of the hand along the palm and fingers without leaving lines caused by overlapping ink impressions, which the smaller rollers almost always leave. The paper, ink and roller can be purchased at any large art shop, and the square of rubber can usually be purchased at stationers' shops.

You can make a print in the following way. First roll a small quantity of ink onto a sheet of paper, or onto a square of glass, with the aid of the roller. The ink film should not be too thick, and it should cover an area of about six inches (the width of the ideal roller) and nine inches (about three revolutions of the rolling surface circumference). The roller should then be run up and down over this area three or four times in order to allow it to pick up an even film of ink. Next wipe the hand firmly with a piece of muslin or fluffless cloth to remove superficial oil and moisture, and then run the roller over the entire palmar and finger surface. Care should be taken to make sure that the film of ink is evenly distributed and that the crease lines on the palm are not filled with ink.

When the hand has been satisfactorily inked, it should be placed face down upon the padded paper surface to make the impression. At this stage, when the inked hand is actually resting on the surface of the paper, a certain amount of direct pressure will be required on the back of the hand to ensure that the print includes the whole of the hand surface. Too much pressure will tend to mar the print by smudging or distorting the papillary ridges — especially on the finger tips. Usually it is only necessary gently to smooth down the fingers, put a slight pressure on the thumb (particulary on the second phalange) and to give a firm pressure on what you estimate to be the exact centre of the palm in order to print the concave area below the finger roots and between the ball of the thumb and the outer ridge which is called the percussion. If you find that you must use a great deal of pressure to print this hollow the rest of the hand print will be spoiled, and in such a case it is advisable to insert a few torn sheets of paper under the padding, at about the place where the hollow rests, in order to give a raised receptive surface for the printing.

Another, but certainly more difficult, method is to lift the hand off the pad with the sheet still adhering to it, to turn the hand over so that the sheet is on top, and then gently rub the back of the paper onto the hand at the point above the hollow. Expert prints can be made in this way only after considerable practice. Once you feel sure that the print will be satisfactory you can strip the paper from the hand. Do this as quickly and firmly as possible to avoid smudging. As soon as the print has been completed relevant information, such as the subject's name, age, job, sex, etc., should be written directly onto the print, or a reference number should be attached for filing and cross reference. The print should be left for some hours to dry.

The main characteristics to look for in a good print are evenness of definition and clarity of impression. There should be no smudging, and no tones. Each of the patterns on the finger tips should be clearly discernible, and the quality and inflexion of each 'crease' line should be accurately represented.

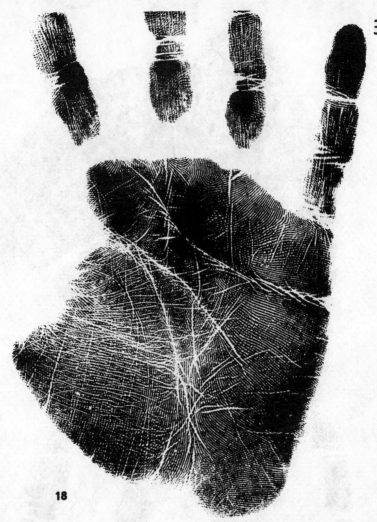

18

18 *A twenty four year old French housewife. The Head line curves in a steady sweep towards the mount of Moon.*

19 *A twenty four year old mathematician. The Head line twists upwards towards the little finger.*

19

1 Line of Life
2 Line of Head
3 Line of Heart
4 Line of Apollo
5 Line of Fate (Saturn)
6 Girdle of Venus
7 Line of Mercury (Intuition)
8 Simian Line

20

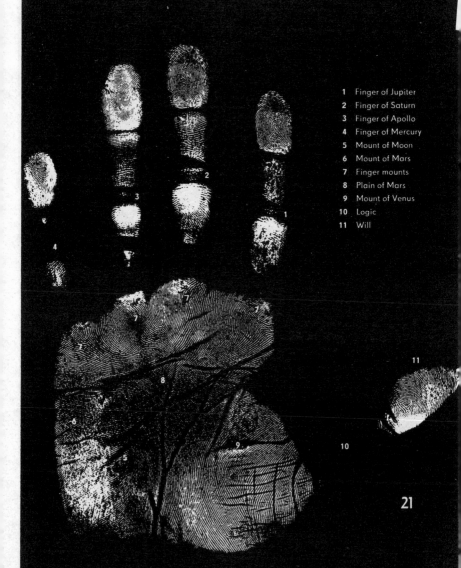

1 Finger of Jupiter
2 Finger of Saturn
3 Finger of Apollo
4 Finger of Mercury
5 Mount of Moon
6 Mount of Mars
7 Finger mounts
8 Plain of Mars
9 Mount of Venus
10 Logic
11 Will

21

22

Once you have prepared a quality print of both of your hands you can proceed with the business of learning the names of the lines and areas of the hand. Plate 20 sets out the names of the major lines on the hand, and indicates the more common subsidiary lines which are not always found on the hand. Try to locate these lines (where they exist) on your own hand, then commit them to memory. The significance of these lines will be discussed later. Plate 21 sets out the names of the major divisions of the hand, as have been established within the tradition of palmistry. These names, as we might expect, are not completely without meaning, and do to some extent throw a light on certain ideas behind palmistry. These names, too, must be committed to memory, and it will be wise to memorize the alternative names, where they exist, as some books on palmistry use slightly different nomenclatures, and it will be useful to know these names should you wish to further your studies by additional reading.

The following notes about the lines of the hand are worth committing to memory at this stage. The Life line is the least variable of all the lines — it always runs around, and in fact demarcates, the third phalange of the thumb which, in palmistry, is called the mount of Venus. The Head line varies both in its point of origin (though usually on or near to the beginning of the Life line) and in its point of insertion, which may be either well down on the mount of Moon (for example plate 18) or well up under the mount of Mercury (for example plate 19). The Heart line always starts at the foot of the mount of Mercury, but its point of insertion varies enormously. Sometimes it runs into the line of Head (to form what is called the Simian line) as can be seen in plate 20, and sometimes it runs deep and well-formed into the space between the fingers of Jupiter and Saturn. On a few hands, as we shall see later, the lines of Head and Heart link to form only one line, which is a severe form of the Simian line (plate 23). The line of Saturn, or the line of Fate as it is sometimes called, runs up the centre of the hand. Although it is regarded as a major line by most palmists, it is very often absent on hands. The various subsidiary lines will be dealt with in a more appropriate place.

In order to start out in a simple way I have so far suggested that you examine only your own hand, but as the whole art of palmistry revolves around comparison — around an attempt to establish relationships between the varying factors in the hand — it is necessary that even in these early stages you gain a degree of familiarity with other hands. In this way you will arrive at some practical idea of what is 'normal', and you will eventually be able to gauge the fine degress of deviation from the norm. It would be very difficult, for example, for you to determine the significance of the Heart line at plate 22, which terminates well between the fingers of Jupiter and Saturn, unless you are familiar with the great variety of terminations of which this line is capable. Because of these considerations, and because of the particular manner in which we are about to study the hand, it will be of considerable help to your study if you can take the hand prints of one or two of your friends in order to compare and contrast them with your own as you build up your analysis.

20 The lines of the hand.
21 The parts of the hand.
22 *A thirty five year old manager. The line of Heart runs into the gap between the fingers of Jupiter and Saturn.*

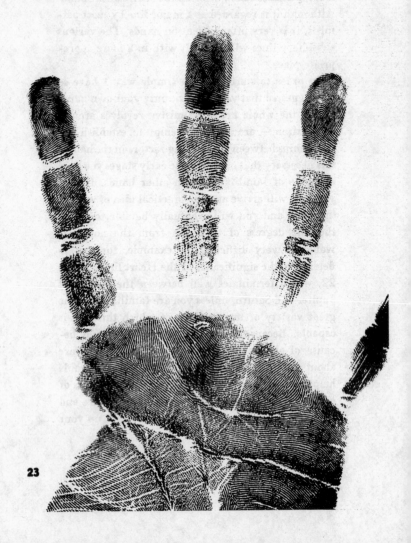

23

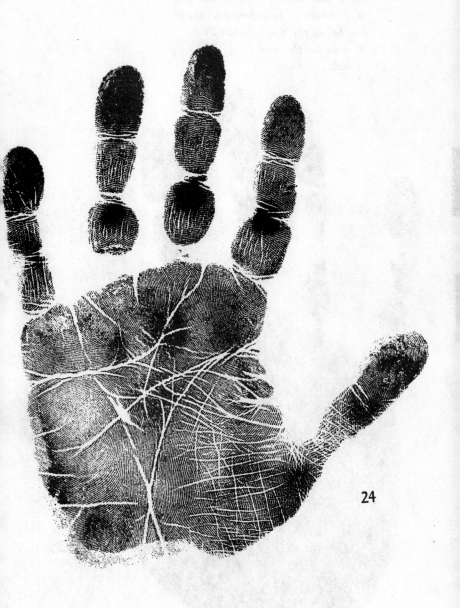

24

23 *An eighteen year old boy. It is best to think of this simian line, which runs across the whole of the hand, as a joining together of the lines of Head and Heart, though one can see remnants of both these lines above and below the main simian line.*

24 *A male Earth hand.*

25 *A male Air hand.*

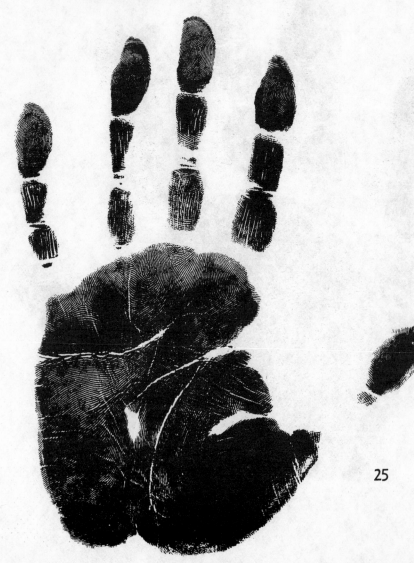

25

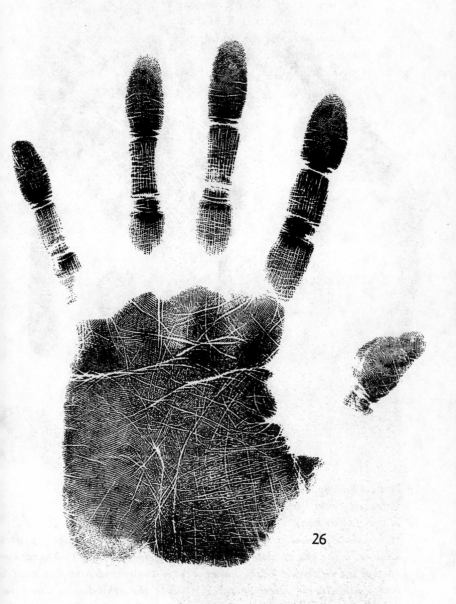

26

27

26 *A male Fire hand.*
27 *A female Water hand.*
28 *A female Fire hand.*
29 *A female Air hand. Compare this
    hand with the one at plate 28, and
    observe the differences in the spaces
    between the fingers. The wide spaces
    exhibited in this print are fairly
    typical of the extrovert personality,
    whilst the fingers held close together
    are an indication of an introverted*
*personality. The finger patter…
themselves on these two hands co…
firm these tendencies, as plate ?…
shows the exhibitionist whorl pa…
terns, whilst plate 28 shows the mo…
restrained loop patterns, except f…
the finger of Jupiter, which is mo…
of an arch.*

For the sake of simplicity it will be advisable to limit the number of prints you take to four or five, and to make your choice of hands in such a way as to give as great a variety of personality types as possible. In making this selection consider carefully the type of personality which you imagine your friends possess, and, working on the principle that greatly different characters will have greatly different hands, make your choice.

On pages 45 to 48 you will find four hand prints which have been especially selected to help you in this difficult business of establishing contrasts as a preliminary step to learning about palmistry. These prints have each been taken from the hands of well-known individuals, all of very different basic temperaments, and yet all related in the sense that they earn their livelihoods either on the Stage or on Television. The prints were taken by me to illustrate a short popular article on palmistry for a woman's magazine, with a special view to introducing the four basic hand types upon which this particular system of palmistry is based. These four prints are therefore especially suitable for our present purpose in that they present a wide range of hand forms and are at the same time a fair representation of the types we shall study. A general analysis of these four hands, which is a copy of the simple analysis I originally did for the magazine before it was put into popular jargon, will be found on pages 138–145 of this book. If you can resist the temptation, it will be as well to read these analyses later, when you will have a more practical working knowledge of palmistry. It should be possible for you yourself to build up an accurate assessment of the character of these four individuals from their hands by the time you have read this book.

Meanwhile, before consulting the readings on pages 138 to 145, try two experiments with these prints. Try, in the first instance, to look at these prints 'emotionally', resisting any attempt to make an intellectual analysis. Try to catch the 'feeling' of these hands: do not force anything, but simply register what your emotions tell you about the hand prints, and perhaps make a few notes as a help to your memory. Try to establish a system for this intuitive palmistry, even at this early stage. Sit down in a comfortable chair, open the book before you and cover all the prints except the one you wish to examine with a sheet of paper. Try to relax your body as much as possible, and to regularize your breathing by filling your lungs slowly with air and then expelling the air equally slowly three or four times. Provided you are relaxed, and your posture is correct, the breathing will help you to intensify the quality of your emotional understanding.

When you feel emotionally alert, look at the print. At this point your mind will start trying to force all sorts of ideas upon you — try to discount the mind, let it chatter on in its own way, and make some attempt to register what you feel about the hand. After only a little practice you will be astonished to find that you have a very useful tool for investigating the world which you have probably not used at all until now. The secret of this method lies in posture and relaxation, but these two, without the ability to discount the chatter of the mind and to register the quiet though insistent voice of the emotions, are of little value.

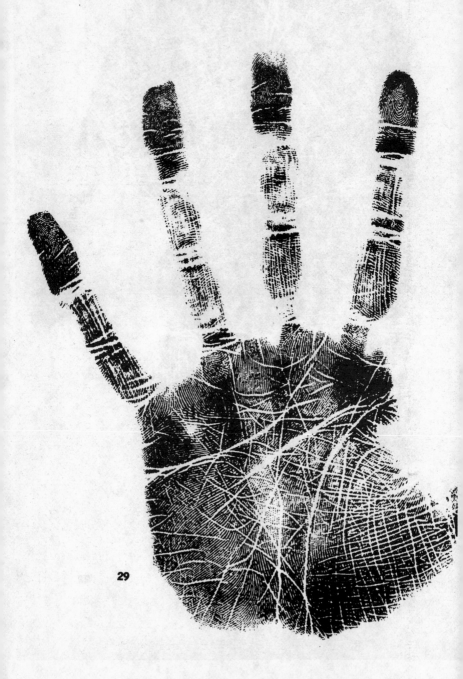

29

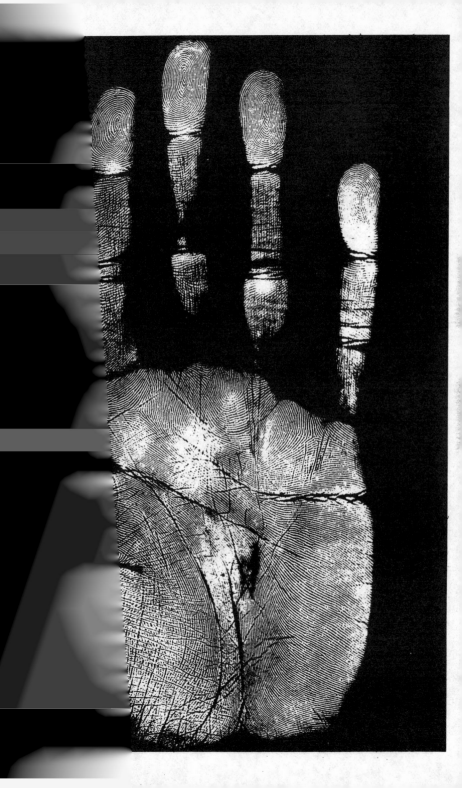

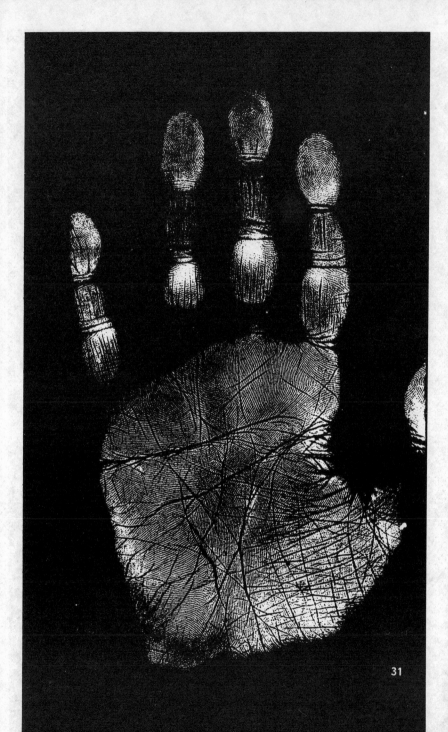

31

This attempt to establish an 'intuitive' understanding of the hand is, of course, related to the second
kind of palmistry which I mentioned in the introduction to this book (page 17). It is a most powerful method of grasping character, and the effort required in
the beginning to refine the emotional sensistivity so
vital to this kind of work is almost always well re-
warded. However much one understands emotionally about palmistry it is always necessary to
be emotionally attuned to the print or hand which
you are examining, and constantly to make experimental sallies with this intuitive method, for with its
aid an enormous amount can be learned both about
the subject under analysis and about yourself.

The second experiment with these four prints can
actually be conducted whilst studying this book.
Each time you read a chapter — or even a complicated paragraph for that matter — you can make
a mental summary of what you have learned, and
then apply this new knowledge to the four prints. In
this way not only will you learn more easily to apply
the analytical form of palmistry, you will also discover the extent to which comparison of details and
forms is the basis of palmistry. Gradually, as you
read the book and apply your knowledge in this way
you will build up a picture of the temperaments
possessed by the four people whose hands have been
reproduced along with a repertoire of palmistic ideas
which can be applied to other hands. Perhaps you
would like to make detailed notes as you go along —
comparing your 'analytical' findings with your 'intuitive' estimates, and finally comparing both these
with the readings on page 138 to 145. It will be
interesting to observe how the final intellectual ana-

lysis compares with the intuitive impression you received before you began your detailed analysis through the applications of the principles behind palmistry.

It is intended that you should follow a somewhat similar procedure with the hand prints you have made of your friends. Here, of course, the difficulty will be that you will have no reading to refer to finally against which to check the veracity of your findings. To some extent you may be able to get around this difficulty by discussing with your friend the analysis you have made of his hand in order to determine approximately how closely your own analysis resembles his picture of himself. With such a procedure you must remember that you may well be on rather dubious ground, as the image people hold of themselves is very often at variance with reality. Clearly, if after a serious analysis you come to the conclusion that a subject has a strong tendency to lie, then it will be too much to hope that he will confirm this analysis!

After experiencing a few hundred analyses along the lines outlined above, you will gradually be forced to the conclusion that the first duty of a palmist is to make a fairly rapid summary from the hand simply in order to estimate with a degree of certainty precisely how far he can take the analysis, and how much he can tell the subject.

This last observation leads me to an important point involving a serious and strict warning. Palmistry, being so intimately linked with imagination, superstition and the fear of the unknown, is a very strong force indeed, and it is necessary for the practising palmist to bear this constantly in mind.

Palmistry must not be abused, for this will not only
damage the subject, but will also damage the palmist. Emotions and understanding of the kind required for good palmistry cannot be harnessed to
forces of evil without loss of quality. Predictions of
the future, especially unpleasant predictions such as
those involving such things as an early death or di-
vorce (both of which charlatans are only too eager
to introduce), and even very severe character analyses, can upset certain types of people very deeply,
Try, therefore, to avoid emotional upsets by developing both a sense of compassion for your fellow
human beings, and a sense of humility towards
your own knowledge of palmistry which, at best,
is fallible – and at worst pretentious. If you do not
study palmistry because you are fascinated by the
hand, or by what you can learn about other people,
about life, and (what is more important) about
yourself, then it is perhaps advisable for you not to
study palmistry at all – for any other motive will
be suspicious and, I might say, not worth the effort.

30 *Long fingers on the hand of a civil
    servant.*
31 *Short fingers on the hand of a female
    clairvoyante.*
32 *A square palm on the hand of an
    eleven year old boy.*

The Form of the Hand

As we have already seen, the best way to approach the analytical side of this study is by making an examination of your own hands and those of one or two of your friends. If it is at all possible, pin these prints to a wall near where you are reading, so that you can constantly refer to the individual prints as you read without too much inconvenience. Keep handy a pencil and paper for making notes. Now examine the hands, beginning with a close comparison of the general proportions.

Are your fingers long or are they short? Obviously, there is no standard by which fingers can be measured, so in a sense the question is absurd. However, if we ask the question more precisely we shall see that an answer is possible. Are the fingers long in proportion to the hand as a whole? With such a question we admit that the length of the fingers is intrinsically bound up with the length or size of the palm. In fact we shall find a little later that the relationship between the length and forms of the fingers and palm is fundamental to the whole principle upon which this system of palmistry is based.

Even so, the answer to the question is still not quite so easy as it may at first appear, and ultimately it is only experience which can determine exactly the importance which may be attached to the length of fingers. Clearly it is evident that the fingers in both 24 and 31 may be called 'short', whilst those in 29 and 30 may be termed 'long', but it is quite difficult to determine which hand has the longest fingers and which the shortest. Here we note, of course, that palmistry deals only with proportions, and not with measurements in inches.

Generally speaking, hands with short fingers

belong to people whose judgements are ruled by intuition. Such people are 'feelers' rather than 'thinkers'. They are not given to careful and systematic consideration of problems, and tend to find self-expression in action. They are sometimes over-hasty, and have a special kind of revulsion against detail. They tend to be impatient. Some of their failings revolve around the tendency to act without due consideration of the outcome of their actions.

Long fingers belong to people given to a love for detail. They are usually careful planners who 'think' rather than 'feel' and in fact they tend to be over-cautious about most things – especially where action is concerned. They tend to love system and order, and will only rarely act without due thought and consideration as to the probable outcome of their actions. They like to have a reason for everything.

A little further on we shall examine the individual fingers in a little more detail, but for the moment we need only note the above two rules, formulate them in our own experience, and examine the two general rules concerning the palm of the hand. With these four combined rules we shall be able to determine the basic principles of hand forms in relation to character, at which point the real study of palmistry begins.

The palm, like the fingers, can be regarded as being either long or short, but experience shows that palms may be more adequately described as being either 'square' or 'long'. A square palm (plate 32) has a very distinctive feeling about it which leads to easy recognition. You will see that although the two square palms on the prints at 24 and 32 differ in

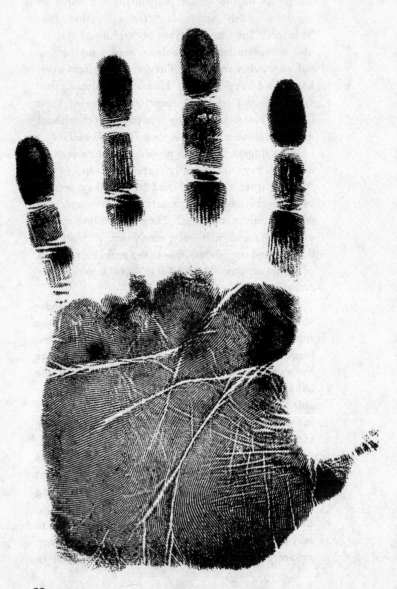

32

33

every other aspect — in texture, weight and linear configuration — none-the-less they each retain a distinctly square quality of shape. This quality will be even more evident when compared with the long palm at plates 27 and 33.

As a generalization we may say that the long palm is a sign of a volatile, even neurotic, personality. The longer the palm the more inclined the personality will be towards an inner emotional unbalance. Check this against your prints by finding the longest palm and considering whether or not the subject is highly strung, neurotic or especially unbalanced. The square palm is a sign of a relatively settled personality. It is rooted in a conservative attitude to life, requiring a sense of security from the person's milieu. Whilst the long palm is fixed in a love for constant change and a certain excitement, and in the pure form ever ready to plunge into the unknown, the square palm grasps at security and certainty.

You will see from the above four generalizations concerning the lengths of the fingers and the shape of the palms, that we have four basic hand types. We may find a square palm with short fingers and a long palm with short fingers, a square palm with long fingers and a long palm with long fingers. If we relate the general characteristics arising from these combinations of fingers and palms we shall find four temperamentally different groupings which form the basis for accurate character analysis. We shall also find that there are other additional characteristics which usually accompany each of these four types and which, to some extent, help in a more exact classification.

At this point it will be very instructive if you can

determine roughly to which of the four groupings each of the hands before you belong. Especially take care in how you classify your own hand — try to look at it as objectively as possible. Do not at this juncture say to yourself. 'I have short fingers, but I know that I like detailed work, so I should in fact take these fingers as being rather long than short!' If you have any doubts about which groupings you should place any of the prints in, look at the four hands on plates 24 to 27, where the classification is fairly obvious, and attempt to estimate which of these prints your own hand resembles in proportion. Once you have satisfactorily classified your hand you can move on to examine a little more closely the psychological implications behind the forms of these hands. If your original choice of prints was based on a sufficiently wide grouping of friends from diverse backgrounds, then you should have at least two, possibly three (and, of course, ideally four) hands representing the types we are about to study.

The first type of hand is the one with a square palm and short fingers. The psychological disposition will be essentially one resulting from a relationship in which judgements are made intuitively (short fingers) with a fairly basic, stable, and balanced emotional background (square palm). The type will, therefore, not be strongly intellectual, and will rely on emotional judgements rather than on mental evaluations. His basic longing for stability will restrict his emotional understanding to some extent, and particularly emphasize his conservative attitude to life. All these factors coalesce to contain his emotional directions within a strictly practical field. Plate 34 is a good example of this type of hand. It is

34

35

33 *A long palm.*
34 *A male Earth hand. The print of
    an Italian.*
35 *A male Air hand.*
36 *A female Fire hand. The print of a
    French female psychologist. Note
    the general "rounding" of the hand
    form so typical of female hands.*

called the *Practical* or *Earth Hand*. There are certain
keywords or key phrases which may be memorized
as being very suitable generalizations which describe
the basic temperament of this type:

> Practical
> Gifted with the hands
> Reliable
> Has his 'feet on the ground'
> Has love for rhythm
> Delights in physical action
> Tends to be possessive
> Steadfast
> Conservative
> Reserved
> Critical and suspicious
> Utilitarian
> Impatient of detail except
> where a craft is concerned
> Penchant for out-of-door work

We shall return to a more detailed investigation
of the hand – particularly in relation to its linear
formations and its complex variant which is called
the *Creative Earth Type* – after we have examined
a little further the principles of palmistry.

The second type of hand is the one with a square palm and long fingers. Here, in order to grasp the essentials of this type, we must picture the love for abstract forms and an intellectual search for self expression (long fingers) and relate these to the basically stable, conservative emotional life represented by the palm. This is the personality type which is constantly reaching out to establish relationships between people and things. His judgements tend to be intellectual, perhaps even a little dry, and indeed, as we shall see in later examinations, there is usually a profound mistrust of emotional values. As in the case of the Practical Type, the square palm will add a strong degree of conservatism, and although the type is extrovert by nature, he will be a little restrained, particularly in establishing emotional relationships. The print in plate 35 is a good example of this type. It is called the *Intellectual* or *Air Type*. The key words and phrases which present a general picture of the temperament of the type are as follows:

Loves communication	Inquisitive
Likes to organize things	Original in mind
Intellectual	Freedom loving
Tends to distrust emotions	Companionable
Needs order in all things	Discriminating
Quick-witted	

The third type of hand is the long palm with short fingers. Here we have a somewhat dangerous combination of a fairly unbalanced emotional life, as indicated by the long palm, combining with a tendency to act freely upon decisions of an intuitive kind, as the short fingers would suggest. This is perforce a very unstable type, given to rapid judgements

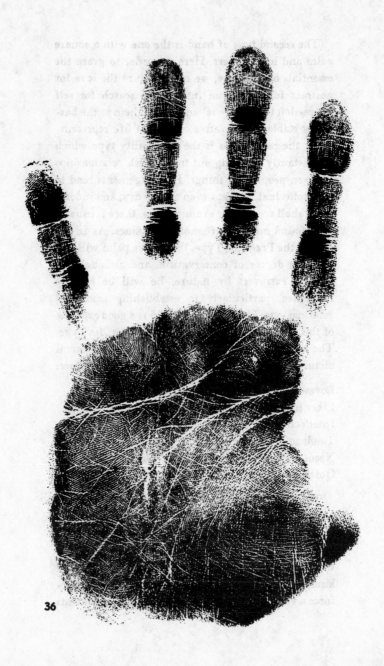

36

37

and equally rapid actions. Much more than the Intellectual type he is extremely extrovert by nature, but his quick emotional life makes him move out towards people very rapidly, and without the conservative restraint of the Air type, with often disastrous results. The print in plate 36 is a good example of the type. It is called the *Intuitive* or the *Fire Hand*. The keywords and key phrases which present a general picture of the type's temperament are as follows:

> Versatile, especially in emotional range
> Warms people with his life
> Full of enthusiasm
> Exciting
> Usually creative
> Must always be active
> Constantly taken up with novel ideas
> Changeable
> Energetic
> Full of initiative
> Dislikes detail
> Egocentric, more than most
> Intuitive rather than intellectual
> Likes to be leader
> Tends to be exhibitionist
> Delights in self-expression

45

*39 Detail from the hand of an Air
type, showing the characteristic
linear patterns of clear main lines
with delicate subsidiary lines.*

*40 Detail from the hand of a Fire type,
showing the characteristic lively
linear patterns.*

41 Detail from the hand of a Water

38

39

type, showing the characteristic mesh
of fine delicate "crease" lines.
42 Although this hand has already been
described as being of the Fire category (see plate 36, where the left
hand is shown) there is a very obvious secondary characteristic indicated by the quality of the lines.

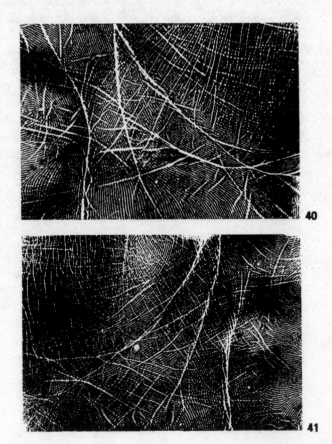

The fourth and last type of hand is the one consisting of a long palm and long fingers. Here the temperament results from a combination of an insecure emotional life, represented by the long palm, and an intellectual abstract attitude to life, as indicated by the long fingers. There is little or no practicality in the type, as all those qualities build up a great feeling of insecurity owing to a rich, but undirected emotional life, and tend to make him withdraw from the world of action. Like the Fire hand, the type exhibits a rather unstable nature, though on the surface he or she may well appear to be fairly contained and peaceable, and the introverted energies do not tend to react quite so quickly, nor do they give rise so readily to direct actions. The type is extremely passive. The print in plate 37 is a good example of this kind of hand. It is called the *Sensitive* or the *Water Hand*. The key words and phrases from which we may draw a general picture of the type are as follows:

Sensitive
Withdrawn
Unstable emotionally
Requires support from others
Secretive
Receptive
Impressionable
Confused, except in field of creativity
Strictly emotional
Idealistic
Fluctuating
'I feel' and not 'I think'.
Requires direction

Likes to be alone
Perceptive within the field of emotions

To add a little to what we have already discussed above, and to clarify the classification a little more, we might make the following observations. The Earth hand is usually heavy and thick, and a print usually shows thick papillary ridges and only a few well-marked crease lines. The type is essentially interested in practical affairs. Under most circumstances (but see page 82) he is stable and contained. His self-expression is given form in changing the outward forms of material things. It might be noted that the type may be of a simple or a complex nature, but this point will be considered fully later on. The hand type is basically masculine. It is most commonly found among mill workers, farmers, labourers, garage mechanics and (in the complex state) among artists of a certain kind.

The Air hand is usually quite soft with reasonably fine papillary ridges on a print, with the main lines well drawn and a variety of weaker subsidiary lines. The type is essentially interested in establishing relationships between people and things, and it is within this domain that he finds his self-expression. His emotional life is stable, though he is fairly extroverted, dampened somewhat by a strong conservative streak. The hand type is equally distributed between male and female, and it is found most commonly among research workers in literary fields, certain types of writers, psychologists, and people whose livelihood is gained by establishing relationships between different entities.

The Fire hand is usually lively in consistency,

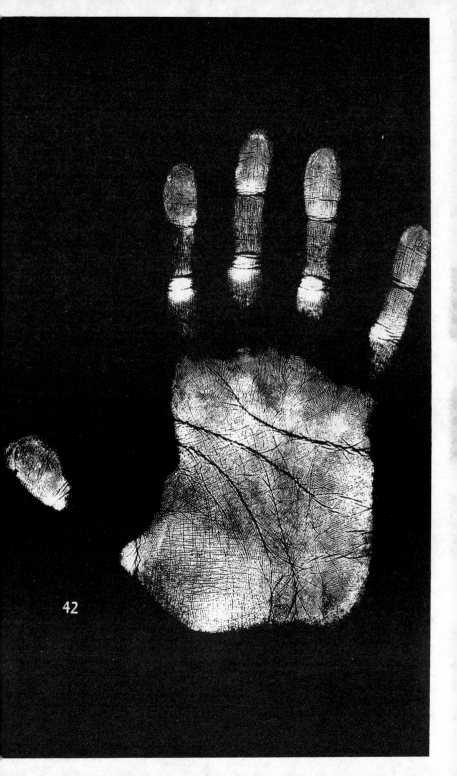

42

43 *A deep set finger of Mercury on the hand of a female social worker.*

44 *A skin growth under the finger of Mercury on the hand of a young Russian with severe sexual problems.*

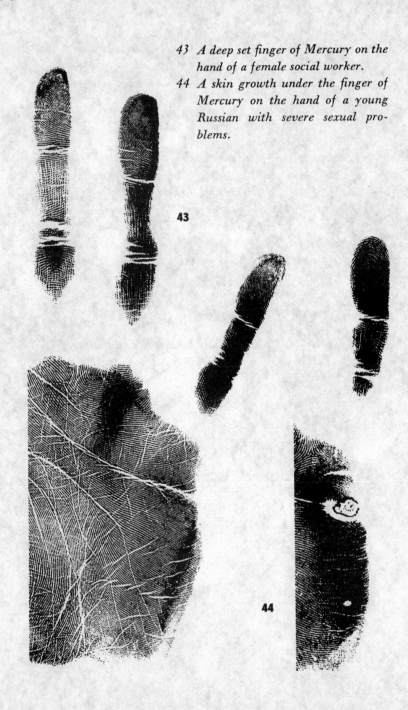

43

44

48

with delicate papillary ridges, and characteristically sharp 'lively' crease lines. The type is essentially interested in a constantly changing field of emotional experiences. His emotional life is extremely unstable and he is changeable and thoroughly extroverted. He is versatile and creative, depending on his intellectual abilities, whilst his self-expression is given form in a wide variety of ways, each characterized by his attempting to impress his own rich personality on a given situation. The hand type is basically masculine in its perfect form, though it is not uncommonly found in certain types of female. The hand is found among artists, energetic businessmen, and such people who easily project themselves into enterprises demanding originality, energy and confidence.

The Water hand is usually delicate in appearance – languid in feeling, with a fine pattern of papillary ridges and a finely etched mesh of crease lines amongst which may be discerned the main lines which are of a very delicate quality. The type is essentially an introverted, insecure personality, with a rich and undirected emotional life. Inwardly unstable and withdrawing, the self-expression occasionally takes the form of deep inner searching within the framework of a religious discipline. As opposed to the Earth hand, from which it differs in every way, the Water hand is feminine in quality. It is frequently found in office girls, certain types of male poets, ballet dancers, actresses, and those who tend to lead a cloistered life.

It is hoped that your knowledge of the temperaments of the friends whose hands you have accepted for analysis is sufficient for you have seen the

underlying truth in some of the above generalizations. It is, however, well worth studying the principles a little more before coming to any hard and
fast conclusion.

I cannot emphasize enough that there is no such
thing as a pure hand type. Each hand manifests
certain traits of every one of the four classifications
in one way or another, but in most instances it is
fairly easy to recognise the predominating type from
the salient characteristics. It is very common indeed
for a hand to manifest two strong type tendencies,
such as Fire and Earth (Fire, for example, in terms
of the finger/palm proportions, and Earth in terms
of the simple strong lines) which clearly indicates
that the type will oscillate between the two extremes
represented by these two directions. Each personality,
every person, lives in a state of tension, and it is
possible to determine the nature of this tension
by finding the two poles between which the temperaments may oscillate. Look at plate 42, for example,
and with your present knowledge of hand forms try
to determine the poles between which the subject
will move. Ask yourself how the central tensions
before the subject will manifest themselves and try
to draw a picture of the subject's type of life. On page
94 you will find my own interpretation of the hand.
with the reasons for this interpretation. You will
note that the subject herself has confirmed the broad
outlines which I indicate in this analysis as being
very accurate. Try to make your own analysis before
consulting my own.

At this point you could also try to determine the
poles of temperament between which the subjects
whose prints you have before you may oscillate.

Check this tentative analysis with each of your friends, to find out how far you are right and wrong. A further exercise will be for you to look once more at the prints on pages 45 to 48 and attempt to determine the secondary poles behind the basic types.

At this juncture we should return to the fingers for a slightly more detailed analysis. We have already noted that the hand may be divided into two areas — the top part of which contains the fingers, the bottom half of which contains the palm. The finger zone relates to the active side of the personality, to those energies which are, in a controlled form, directed towards the outside world. The palmar zone relates to a more passive, contained, side of the personality — more exactly, to those energies which are subconsciously controlled.

It is because of this that the fingers give a clue as to how the subject will manifest in a wide variety of fields — especially within the field of personal relationships.

A further division of the hand may be made by drawing a line down the centre, as in plate 45. Such a division leaves us with four quarters, when superimposed over the first division. The percussion half of this second division, which contains the little finger and the ring finger, is regarded as the introverted side of the personality, whilst the other half of the division, containing the middle finger, the index and the thumb, is regarded as the extroverted side of the personality. We thus find that the hand may be thought of as consisting of four quarters, each relating to a specific energy direction.

The quarter which contains the little finger and the ring finger represents the personal and active

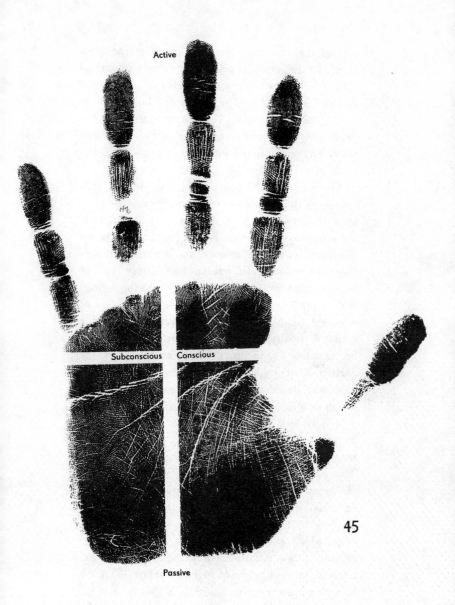

Active

Subconscious Conscious

45

Passive

side of the externally directed energies, and from these two fingers it is possible to draw a picture of some of the more private emotions and directions of the subject's life. The finger of Mercury is, to some extent, representative of the sexual side of the personality, whilst the finger of Apollo is representative of the emotional direction, intensity and balance of the personality.

The finger of Mercury relates to the subject's dealing with the opposite sex, to money and, to a lesser extent, to honesty. A ring on the little finger is almost always a sign of a lack of balance in relation to sex or money, for instance, and it is very interesting that homosexuals, lesbians and certain types of business men 'isolate' this finger by wearing a ring! A deep set finger of Mercury (Plate 43) is a sign of a parent fixation which is often at the root of a sexual difficulty. A skin growth at the root of this finger (plate 44) is also a sure sign of a temporary partner difficulty. In even the very oldest forms of palmistry a twisted little finger has always stood as a sign of a liar or of a criminal degenerate — particularly if, as it sometimes happens, one of the three phalanges is missing on the finger. A long nail phalange is a sign that the subject tends to exaggerate. This does not mean to say that the subject is strictly 'dishonest', but more that his tongue tends to let his imagination run away with him. If the shape of the finger is well formed and smooth, with the top phalange nicely pointed, the subject will be possessed of quite a fine vocal ability in the field of self expression. A bent finger of Mercury (plate 46) is the sign of a 'money-maker', and such a finger has the same significance (taken with other factors in the

45 *The four main areas of the hand.*
46 *A bent finger of Mercury on the hand of a Jewish businessman.*
47 *A callous under the finger of Apollo, indicating severe emotional strain.*

47

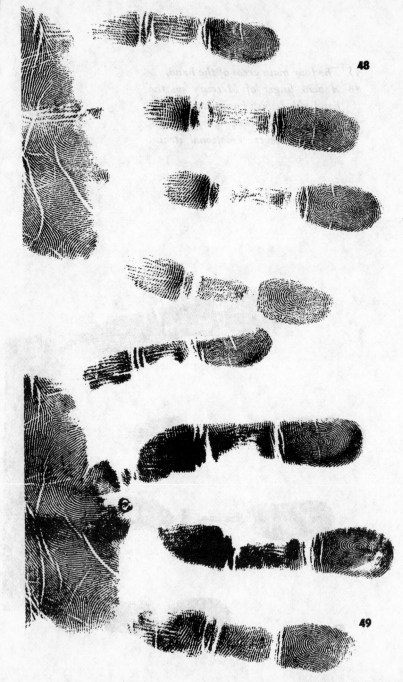

48

49

hand, such as a fairly practical head line, and strong Fire characteristics) as the wearing of a ring — the subject has a persuasive tongue which leads people to part with their money. Such people are especially well adapted for controlling other people.

The only side of the subject's personal life not covered by the finger of Mercury is that which deals with self-expression and with emotional balance. Both these are represented by the finger of Apollo. A ring on this finger is, of course, a statement to the outside world of emotional concord. The quality of the finger related (as we shall see) to the line of Apollo indicates to what extent the subject is contented within the framework of the structure of his life direction. A short finger indicates a tendency of the superficial personality to be completely at loggerheads with his expressed aims. A long finger indicates one too much preoccupied with his emotional problems. In each case emotional factors cloy the creative impulse and destroy actual artistic production. A urge to create, to give form to matter, is indicated by a whorl pattern on the finger (page 96), but one must be careful to evaluate the rest of the hand — especially the line of Apollo, the thumb and the type — before designating the subject as 'creative', for the wish to create may not be complemented by the ability. From a point of view of inner balance, and satisfaction with emotional direction, the finger of Apollo with even length and a square third phalange is to be looked for. You must not forget, however, that 'balance' is a relative term, and what may be regarded as well-balanced behaviour in a Water type would hardly be regarded as such in a Fire type. Never fail to relate the individual significance of minor factors to the whole pattern of the hand type.

The quarter of the hand which contains the other two fingers and the thumb represents the active and externally directed energies of the personality. From the fingers of Saturn and Jupiter it is possible to estimate how the subject will act in his external life.

The finger of Saturn may be thought of as the 'balance-finger' standing, as it does, between the internal personal energies and the external extroverted energies of Jupiter and the thumb. A ring on the finger of Saturn, or for that matter a callous at the finger root (plate 47), indicates a personality with a severe problem of inner adjustment: the conflict between the inner world and the outer world will manifest itself in some definite form. The personality given as an example at plate 48 is under severe stress, as the energies represented by the percussion half of the hand can find little or no meeting point with the other half. I compare this detail of the print with one made of the same hand about nine months earlier to show that the conflict (which arose after the first impression had been made, and which was, incidentally, forseen in the hand from other factors) was recorded afterwards. It is not possible to show a third detail, with the callous absent, as it will remain for another seven or eight months. A callous or a ring will indicate temporary state of inner tension, but a pattern on the third phalange which is greatly different from the patterns on the other finger tips will indicate a much more permanent state of tension. In some cases such a tension gives rise to a strong creative ability accompanied by a somewhat neurotic personality. Other

48 The hand of an artist.

49 The hand of the same artist as at
plate 48, showing the development
of a callous between the fingers of
Apollo and Saturn indicating considerable difficulty of adjustment to
life. A few days prior to this print
being taken this man had attempted
suicide.

50 A bent finger of Jupiter adding an
acquisitive strain to a hand predominately Earth with strong Fire
characteristics.

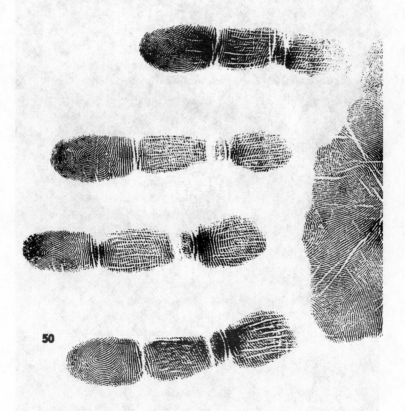

50

tendencies can be determined from the length of the
finger – if, for example, the subject has a long finger of Saturn one can assume that a strong intellectual restriction results in an open conflict between
emotions and intellect. If the subject has an especially short finger (relative, of course, to the other
fingers) one must assume that there is an insufficient
mental control resulting in emotional chaos, and
therefore lack of balance.

The finger of Jupiter is regarded as the indicator
of those externally directed energies of the personality which are easily observed. The finger is sometimes called the 'world-finger' or the 'finger of Ambition'. It certainly gives a fair estimate of the person's attitude to materials things, and so perhaps
neither of these two names is far from the mark.
A bent finger of Jupiter (plate 50) shows a strong
acquisitive tendency and great material ambition.
A short finger of Jupiter (plate 51) is a sure sign of
an inferiority complex – the subject will be easy
going, lacking in self confidence and with a strong
tendency to justify his actions. The long finger of
Jupiter (plate 52) indicates a somewhat overbearing
personality, perhaps a little too sure of himself and
his abilities. Whatever tne length of the finger, a
callous at the root indicates a great inner struggle to
adjust to difficult life circumstances. This is, of
course, an indication of a temporary state of affairs.
The example at plate 53 is to be compared with the
same hand from a print taken a few years after the
subject had solved his life difficulties to some
degree.

It should almost go without saying that the significance of each finger must be related to the hand

as a whole. One quite often finds a fairly short finger of Jupiter on a Water type, and this of course is only an indication of what one would expect in a personality in this grouping. Such a finger would have quite a different significance on a Fire hand.

Some palmists, particularly those who base their methods on the teachings of Desbarolles, the nineteenth century French chiromancer, place a great deal of emphasis on the meanings to be perceived in the finger endings. It is suggested by such palmists that the actual silhouette of the finger end, viewed from the front or back, determines certain aspects of the subject's character. In my own experience this teaching is not really well founded. Each finger has its own characteristic termination: the finger of Mercury is usually pointed, the finger of Apollo is usually slightly spatulate, the finger of Saturn almost square and the finger of Jupiter usually rounded. However, it must be admitted that the whole hand usually manifests a tendency on the part of the fingers to conform to a certain 'shape' of squareness, etc., and this serves as a guide to some of the more subtle relationships behind the basic type. The fingers of the Fire hand are usually rounded, lithe and subtle. The fingers of the Earth hand are usually square in cross section, heavy, hard, knotted and thick. The fingers of the Water hand are usually quite graceful, smooth, round in cross-section and gentle to the touch. The fingers of the Air hand are usually quite graceful, smooth and well proportioned, though never as thin or refined as the Water fingers. There is a tendency of the Air type to hold the fingers fairly widely apart – especially on prints. If, as occasionally

51 *A short finger of Jupiter.*
52 *A long finger of Jupiter.*
53 *A callous under the finger of Jupiter.*
54 *The same hand as at plate 53 a few years later.*
55 *An overbearing thumb.*
56 *A strong thumb.*
57 *A bulbous thumb.*

53

54

happens, you should find a hand which essentially Fire in its basic proportions, but with fingers and palm indicating strong Earth tendencies (plate 19, for example), then you must carefully attempt to evaluate the degree to which the struggle between Fire and Earth are manifest in the subject's life.

Try at this stage to determine the basic conflicts in the life of each of the subjects whose hands you have undertaken to study. You can do this fairly simply by determining the poles of conflict from the basic type (palm/finger proportions) and the direction of energies (indicated by the character of the lines – see plates 38 to 41 for examples). If you find a basic Water hand with strong Fire lines then your picture must be one in which a basically retiring and insecure type is continually (the frequency will depend on the strength of the lines) being made to 'boil' by its Fire polarity. An Earth hand with, say, strong Fire lines would be a strange conflict of poles in which practicality would be backed by a bubbling versatility – this type of hand is not uncommon in artistic circles. Before you move on to study further, make an attempt to discover the poles between which your selected subjects move.

The thumb is divided into three parts by palmists. The nail phalange is usually called the phalange of Will, the second is refered to as the phalange of Logic, and the third part, the heavy ball of the thumb, is called the mount of Venus. The top two phalanges of the thumb are located in that part of the hand which relates to conscious life and, in connexion with the finger of Jupiter and the line of Life (page 122) may be taken as representing the vital energy of the subject.

As a preliminary generalisation we might say that a large thumb indicates a forceful personality. Look at the print before you and try to determine who has the largest thumb (that is, of course, in relation to the hand as a whole). It will be rather difficult to tell directly from a print, as the thumb rarely prints well, so you must make a note to try to find from direct examination of the hands which of them is the largest. You can be sure that the type will be either Fire or Earth! Try to find in this one hand what two or more poles produce a basic conflict of temperaments and you will be certain that with such a large thumb this conflict will manifest itself in some direct physical way.

The phalange of Will, the nail phalange, indicates the manner in which the subject's basic energies are directed towards the outside world. A narrow Will phalange, either narrow or pointed, indicates that the energies run very freely and not too strongly from the subject. Personalities with such thumbs tend to be unable to make decisions readily, or to act on their decisions once they have made them. This type of thumb is, as one might expect, usually found in its pure aspect on a Water hand where it is 'true to type'. A similar thumb on a Fire hand would be very dangerous, for the resulting conflict between Water and Fire at such an important junction as the outlet of energies would very much impair the inner harmony of the person and might well be destructive in the long run.

A strong, well-balanced, phalange of Will is a sign of a healthy outlet of energies. The subject will quickly (though perhaps too quickly) translate emotions into actions. Such a thumb it typical of the

Fire hand, though it is often found also on the Air type.

A bulbous phalange of Will, which is somewhat histrionically described by some palmists as the 'Murderer's thumb', belongs to none of the pure types. It has a characteristic form which is easily recognised and 'felt'. No one can examine such a thumb without feeling the repression of energies which the form conveys. It is an atavistic sign which almost always indicates a strong involutary force within the subject. If it may be said to be characteristic of any of the four types at all, it must be placed within the Earth type, which has the largest incidence of atavistic signs such as missing phalanges, deformed thumbs and strong simian lines (page 118). The clubbed thumb, with its attendant repressions, on a coarse hand of the Earth type is a sign of a badly controlled temper. Such a thumb as this is fairly rare, and it is unlikely that you have one in your present collection.

The second phalange, which is called the phalange of Logic, indicates something of the restraint with which reasoning power may invest ultimate action. A large and thick phalange will be a sign of considerable care and thought with regard to the outcome of definite actions – though a phalange of great thickness and length tends to be a killer of action. A waisted second phalange indicates an impulsive direction of energies almost devoid of control. Such a phalange with a heavy joint or with a heavy phalange of Will indicates a personality completely committed to impulsive actions. The knot between these two phalanges is a sort of manifestation of the relationship between the control

55

56

57

58 The arch pattern.
59 The loop pattern.
60 The whorl pattern.
61 An enlarged complex finger pattern.
    The single triadus, which marks
    this down as a loop pattern, can be

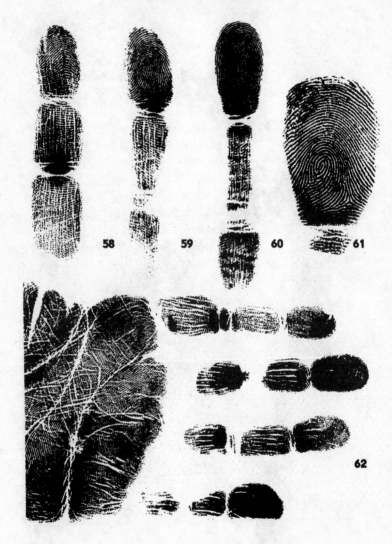

seen to the right of the print, as a
triangular area of white containing
three black ridges meeting at a point
in the centre of the triangle.
62 One hand exhibiting three different
finger patterns.
63 A hand with loop patterns on each
finger. The direction of the loop on

and manifestation of energies. A large knot will result in an unevenness of application: the person possessed of such a joint will find it difficult to complete a task which he has undertaken.

If you continue to study thumbs with both an intuitive direction and an intellectual direction you will gradually be able to build up a useful system of references as to the distinctive feelings which certain types of thumbs evoke. One of the first things you should do when you have determined the basic type and/or temperamental conflicts of the personality is to find out whether or not his life manifestations are strong or weak, tending to dominate or tending to be reticent, and whether or not he is capable of bringing to a conclusion those projects which his energies encourage or force him to undertake. These factors can best be evaluated by examination of the thumb, the finger of Jupiter and the Head line.

Considerable practice is required to begin to sense the importance of the fingers and thumb, but it will be found that they contain within their form the very essence of those psychological dispositions which form the complicated structure of a given personality.

> *the finger of Jupiter is fairly com-*
> *mon — this is the radial loop.*
>
> *64 A hand with whorl patterns on each*
> *finger. This is usually an artistic*
> *hand if found on the fire type, but*
> *it is always a sign of a very sensitive*
> *personality.*
>
> *65 A richly lined Air hand.*

The form, length and quality of the individual fingers apart, there are two other factors which may contribute towards building up an analysis of the subject's personality. I refer to the finger patterns and the nails.

The finger patterns on prints are the traces in ink left by the delicate papillary ridges on the top phalanges. These patterns are of considerable importance to the palmist, and great care should be taken in order that correct indentification of each of these patterns be made before committing yourself to a detailed character analysis.

Although the construction of these finger patterns vary enormously — and it is said that no two are alike in the whole world — there are only three basically different patterns. The simplest is called the Arch (plate 58), the one a little more complex is called the Loop (plate 59), and the most complex of all is called the Whorl (plate 60).

In their simplest forms each of these patterns can be fairly easily identified, but when there is any doubt it is as well to look for the triadus (see plate 61) which is a sort of triangular island serving to relate the main pattern to the series of parallel papillary ridges above the first finger crease. The

triadus will be found to be a useful guide to the identification of the patterns. An Arch has no triadus, as it is merely a raised extension of these parallel ridges. A Loop has one triadus, found directly under the belly of the loop, whilst the Whorl stands quite isolated from the parallel ridges by two triadii.

The Arch is found most frequently on the finger of Jupiter and on the Earth hand type, and this to some extent reflects the characteristics which this pattern represents. The Arch is a sign of a certain basic crudeness of sensitivity, which is counterbalanced by practicality. When the Arch is found on many or all fingers on a hand we can expect the subject to be somewhat rebellious by nature. A mixture of 'no-nonsense' practicality and open suspicion tends to create a 'Bolshie' personality often at loggerheads with the milieu in which he finds himself. A list of keywords worth remembering for this pattern would be along the lines of 'rebellious, stubborn, defiant and ambitious in a practical way'.

The Loop pattern is by far the commonest. The Ulnar loop (plate 63), with loop emerging from the percussion side of the hand is very common, and is the sign of a fairly subdued unoriginal personality – especially when found on all the fingers. The keywords to bear in mind for this pattern are 'clear-spirited, cool and reflective in judgement, restraint in self-expression'. The Radial loop (plate 63) is much more rare than the Ulnar, but occurs most frequently on the finger of Jupiter. It is a sign of individuality within the field of life endeavour, and though it is not a creative pattern it does suggest that a certain unique bearing will distinguish the subject either in the form of attitude to life or in conduct. The keywords would be much the same as those for the Whorl type but in a slightly more restrained and less creative sense.

The Whorl pattern is often found in isolation on the finger of Apollo and, less frequently, on the finger of Mercury. It is the sign of a restless, creative, though somewhat vacillating type with a strongly developed ego. One pure Whorl on the finger of Apollo indicates a deep wish for self-expression — it should not be too difficult to work out whether or not the hand type and such other factors as the line of Apollo indicate that this wish is easily satisfied. The hand with a whorl pattern on all fingers (plate 64) is fairly rare — such a hand will almost certainly be a Fire type, though sometimes one does find an Air type in this category (plate 89 for instance). A type with pure Whorl on all fingers will be a 'law unto himself', with a brilliant creative urge which is sometimes too widely diffused, too versatile. He will be eager for action, clever and egocentric in a very open way. The keywords for this pattern are 'Versatile, restless, egocentric and creative'.

It should be clear from the above notes that the Arch pattern tends to add a degree of Earth qualities to the hand, the Loop pattern tends to add a degree of Water qualities and the Whorl pattern tends to add a degree of Fire. It is worth bearing this in mind even at the preliminary stage of your analysis.

A worthwhile experiment will be for you to draw up a picture of each of the hands you have before you solely in terms of the finger patterns —

relating each pattern to the significance of the individual finger. You can then take this reading and regard it as an indication of the opposite polarity to the hand type as read from the hand form itself. If the reading is not in any way opposed to the general reading from the chirognomy of the hand, then you must take it that the direction of the subject is too intense and lacking in balance. In such a case you will be faced with a very strong personality indeed.

Very many generalizations have been made in the past about the significance of the nails. Indeed, whole books have been written about the subject of the importance of nails in palmistry, and this has tended to place undue emphasis on precisely what one can infer from the quality of the nails. In my own experience the following generalizations are the only reliable ones. Narrow nails (essentially feminine in quality) indicate a fairly weak physical strength. They are most frequently found on Water hands and female Air hands. Short nails are a sign of a critical disposition, and the reading must be made in terms of the hand form upon which the nails are found — a series of short, coarse and heavy nails on an Earth hand will add a critical tendency to a personality already disposed to a natural suspicion and will obviously have a different meaning from similar nails on a Fire of Water hand. Heavy, thick (and very often fluted) coarse nails are found on the pure Earth hand. Long, delicate and narrow nails are found on the pure Water hand. Square, medium-sized nails are found on the Fire hand. Large open nails are found on the male Air hand, whilst longish delicate nails are found on

the female Air hand. Each of these nail characteristics will impart a degree of the qualities of the type to which they are common.

The lower half of the hand contains the mount of Moon on the percussion side, and the mount of Venus which is the lower phalange of the thumb. Between them they represent two different forms of energy. Moon relates to the passive subconscious energies, whilst Venus relates to the more direct energies which actually manifest themselves in life.

The mount of Moon may be considered the seat of the sensitive psychic qualities. If the Moon is well developed, which is to say fairly fleshy or particularly marked with papillary ridge patterns, then you may expect the sort of imagination which leads to romantic dreams of an escapist nature. A strong downward curve of the line of Head will confirm this tendency. Such a mount is, however, a complement to the creative faculties, should these be observed elswhere in the hand, as a developed mount is not necessarily uncreative.

The mount of Venus relates to a more externally directed energy — a firm, well-rounded mount is a sign of good health and a powerful supply of energy. The sex drive is usually strong — and a much rayed mount such as the one at plate 91 indicates a quick passage of strong creative energies into life. Such markings are always found on the really creative hand. An undeveloped mount of Venus is not so much a sign of a poor or weak constitution so much as an indication that vital energies are somewhat reserved, and rarely find an outward expression.

We have now considered most of the generalisations which may be made with certainty about the chirognomy of the hand. It will be a useful step to look at each of the hands before you and, purely from memory, run through the facts you can recall as being relevant to each particular hand. Start with the palm — is it long or square? Are the fingers long or short? Are the lines of the type you would expect on that form of hand? What are the main papillary ridge qualities? What are the finger patterns? Are there any forms which catch your attention particularly? Is there an excessive gap between any of the fingers? Is Jupiter long or short? How about Mercury — is it longer than usual? Rehearse these questions, and make attempts to answer them. Perhaps you have the sort of mind which would like to make a certain order around which you can establish each of your analyses. If so work out each of the main chirognomical factors in order of appearance — bearing in mind always just to what degree one characteristic may affect another. Try to make a balance in your judgements.

It will be worthwhile doing a chirognomical analysis of each of your hands to submit to the friends who allowed you to make prints. Discuss these analyses with them, but point out that certain factors which may be revealed by the line patterns have not yet been taken into account.

When you feel confident that you have mastered the simple elements of palmistry as set out in the above few pages, you can move on to the next section which deals with the chiromancy of the hand.

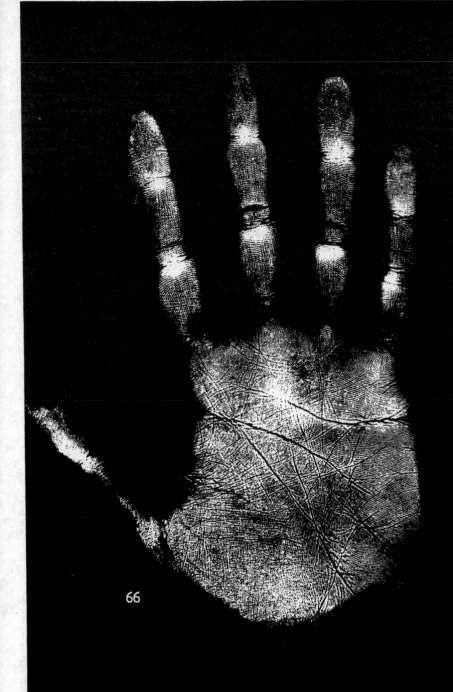

66

The lines of the Hand

WE have already noted that the lines of the hand
vary a great deal, and that there is a marked relationship between the form of the hand and the
linear characteristics — that, for example, it is reasonable to expect a few strong, rather coarse lines
on a pure Earth hand. Clearly the relationship
between the lines and hand form is very important
and to a certain extent is useful in determining subsidiary characteristics, but in addition to this it is
possible to determine a considerable amount about
the subject's personality by studying the 'pattern'
of the lines on the hand. Before we begin to examine
examples of such patterns there are one or two generalizations which are worth making concerning the
lines.

The lines of the hand, unlike the papillary ridges,
can and do change. Considerable fluctuation is fairly
rare however, and it usually takes a detailed study
of prints separated in time by many years to note
any significant change. The changes themselves
parallel, of course, changes in personality traits —
we have already seen how the development of
callouses are significant of inner changes.

Breaks in lines are not necessarily unpleasant
signs. As you begin to practice palmistry you will
find that people are constantly referring to 'breaks
on the Life line' which they believe (possibly as a
result of what some professional or amateur palmist
has said) heralds an early and unpleasant death. It
will be your duty as a serious palmist to clear up this
point and to assure them that although a break *may*
(and only *may*) relate to a trauma of some kind, it
does not, and can not, refer to death.

It is helpful to think of the lines as conductors of

energies from one part of the hand to another – so that, for example, you may consider the Heart line as running along a course which divides the active and passive halves of the hand, transferring energies from the introverted half to the extroverted half. In a hand with a badly chained Heart line (plate 68) on the percussion side of the line you can assume that the emotional source lacks clarity – emotions will be very mixed, complicated and rich in calibre. If such emotional qualities are carried (by the main Heart line) towards, say, the finger of Jupiter, with a general simplification of linear characteristics as in plate 70, you can assume that the complex energies find a fairly ambitious outlet, are channelled from the incipient confusion into a steady direction. You can see from this example that the direction, quality and termination of the line must always be considered together.

The examples of line characteristics at plate 38 to 41 will give you some idea of the basic qualities which certain lines represent. Do not forget that what may well be regarded as 'healthy' lines in one type of hand (plate 38 with an Earth hand; plate 41 with a Water hand, for example) may be quite dangerous on another hand type. The lines actually indicate the state of flux which exists between the psyche of the individual, and the world within which the individual lives – it is a mark of his life pattern.

66 *The hand of a male designer.*

67 *A male Fire hand, with simple Earth lines. The hand of a sailor.*

68 *A chained head line. There is a slight fork at the end.*

The Line of Head

THE length of the headline will give you a clue to
the scope of the subject's intelligence. It is perhaps a
dangerous generalization to say that the longer the
line is the more intelligent the person may be ex-
pected to be, for an extremely long line may run
well down the hand (as at plate 66) and finish up in
the depths of the mount of Moon. In such a case
a very wide intellectual scope would be lost in excessive imagination (consider the result of intellectual energies being poured into the unreal world of
the imagination, with its inevitable result of a lack
of mental balance).

A line of head which runs in a straight course
across the palm (plate 67) indicates the practical,
matter-of-fact intellectual attitude. Concentration
will be quite good — especially if the quality of the
line is clean and fresh. If the line curves up slightly
at the end there will be a somewhat excessive practical twist to the intellect, which adds a lack of sym-
pathy for other people — it is a sign not so much of
an over egoistical attitude so much as of an inability
to take other people into consideration.

Sometimes one finds a fork in a headline (plate
68) with one line running upwards or outwards
towards the higher percussion, and with the other
line running down towards the mount of Moon.
This is always an interesting sign, for it indicates a
personality with the type of intellect which can see
two points of view — the strictly practical and the
strictly imaginative. Such a personality will live in a
strange world — he will find it difficult to tell the
truth, for example, not from an innate dishonesty,
but rather from an inability to determine exactly
what the truth is. The world of the imagination

67

68

69 *A fire hand of a young boy.*

70 *A fire hand with the strong head line separated from the line of Life.*

71 *A spanish female fire hand, with line of Heart finishing between the fingers of Saturn and Jupiter. The mother of eleven children.*

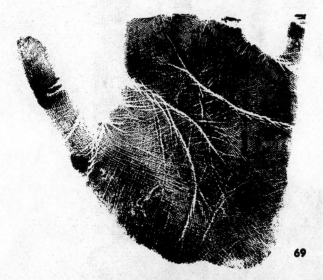

69

will be just as 'real' as the world of practicality. People with such forks are not only interesting for their dual attitude to life – they are usually very very intelligent, and with this gift of being able to see two sides of a problem they are usually in a good position to advise others. Unfortunately their 'dual intelligence' leaves them very confused about most things – especially if they are strong emotional types.

Although it is reasonable to expect a strong curve

70

of the Head line towards Moon in a Water hand, we must on the whole regard such a line as a dangerous sign. The deeper the curve the more unpractical the personality, the more removed from the commonly accepted world of 'reality'. In a creative hand such a line will be a useful adjunct, of course, but even here the excessive imagination can have a disturbing influence on the person's mental balance.

A chained line of Head (plate 68) is an indication of bad concentration – whatever the length or source of such a line you must read 'lack of intellectual application' into the subject. The chaining of the line will echo the mental application of the subject. His attention will fluctuate in direction even though the course and length of line indicates a good strong, practical intelligence.

The importance of the course of the Head line is best considered in relation to the Life line. When the line springs from the Life line, after running with it either in a tangled chain or as one steady line (plate 69), one can assume that the subject will be very cautious about making decisions. Such a commencement will be a good sign in a business man, provided the line is not too chained, and provided that its coarse suggests a reasonable practicality. This sort of commencement usually manifests itself in a kind of shyness and lack of confidence. When the line starts above the line of Life, further up towards Jupiter (plate 70), one can assume a certain open confidence, a ready judgement and independent attitude towards life. This commencement is a good sign of an Air characteristic in mental attitude. It is very commonly found on the Air hand.

71

72 *The hand of a seven year old boy.*
The line of Heart actually finishes
below Saturn, though the Girdle of
Venus might suggest that it termin-
ates between the two fingers. Usually
the difference in quality between
these two lines enables one to per-
ceive where the line of Heart finishes
and the Girdle begins.

73 *A strong Girdle of Venus.*

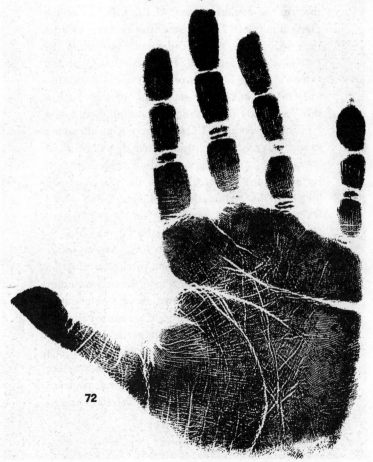

72

The Line of Heart

THE length of the Heartline will lend a clue to the scope of the subject's emotional calibre. The longer the line, the warmer the personality, the more human and understanding. The course of the line indicates the subject's attitude to sex. If the line runs in a steady, unbroken sweep from below Mercury between the fingers of Jupiter and Saturn (plate 71) you can assume the person to have a healthy, physical attitude to sex. On the other hand, should the line terminate in a swing downwards towards the commencement of the Life line or the Head line (plate 73) the resulting coldness of attitude will add a strong degree of idealism to the emotional considerations. In a male hand one can expect a strong female streak, not only in the attitude to sex, but in all emotional matters. Such a line on a male Fire hand, for example, will add a very strong feeling of insecurity, not at all proper to such a type. Such a line on a female hand will, of course, indicate strong masculine tendencies – a certain coldness unbecoming to the sex. A strong break in the termination of a Heart line which finishes on Jupiter or well between the two fingers, or a fork at the termination (plates 72 and 73) indicates a force of inconsistency which may be interpreted as a flirtatious disposition (with a termination between the fingers) or of a cold dispassionate nature (with a termination down under the mount of Jupiter). As a basic simplification we can say that the curve of the Heart line is the important characteristic – the curve will indicate human warmth, a wish to love, and a wish to be loved in return; whereas the straight path is significant of an independence and coldness which does not seek close relationships.

Just as a chained Head line indicates lack of mental concentration, so a chained Heart line indicates lack of emotional concentration. The richness of the chaining, the changing of direction and the 'fluffiness' of the Heart line at plate 74 indicates, for example, not only a state of some emotional instability, but also (and perhaps a result of the instability) a degree of inconstancy and fickleness which is hardly conducive to a steady relationship with another person.

The Girdle of Venus is a kind of subsidiary to the Heart line. A strong Girdle, such as the one at Plate 73, indicates a restless emotionality, and is found on the type of person who is constantly caught in a state of imbalance. It is difficult for a person with a strong Girdle to settle down to a steady job of work or to find any lasting position of security either in life or within himself. The Girdle is a sign of a constant search for new experiences — the personality may well want security with a part of himself, but the very nature of his being drives him into undertakings and emotional attitudes which destroy the possibility of such security. The restless versatility and rich emotionality of the Fire type is increased with a strong Girdle. The instability of the Water type is also increased with a strong Girdle. Air and Earth rarely have pronounced Girdles.

Sometimes the line of Heart meets up with the line of Head, and forms a single line which runs right across the palm. Such a formation is called the Simian line. Plates 74 to 77 indicate the different forms of the Simian line which are most commonly found. In very simple terms the line is a distinct sign of a strong inner tension. The form

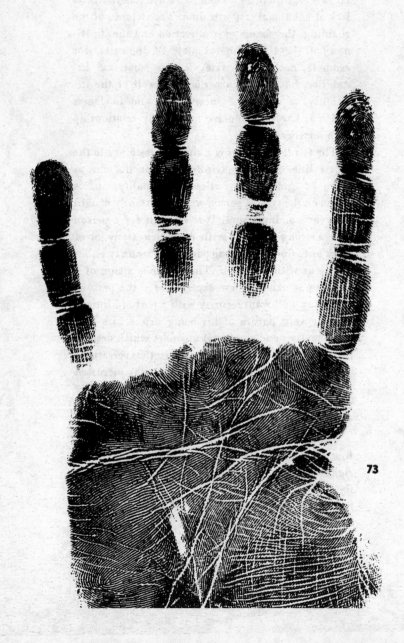

73

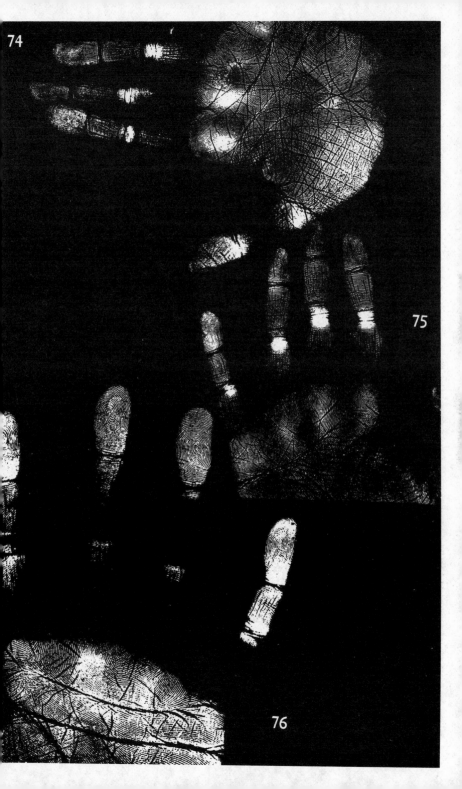

74 The hand of an eight year old boy. The lines springing from the termination of the line of Heart towards the line of Head are called incipient Simian lines.

75 The left hand of the same boy as at plate 74. The incipient Simian lines are even more numerous than on the right hand.

of the hand, along with certain other characteristics, will indicate how this strong tension will manifest itself. In a hand with criminal tendencies (such as a coarse Earth hand) the tension will be manifest in explosive actions of a destructive nature – the line is found very often on the hands of people fond of fighting, for example. In a hand with creative tendencies (such as a refined Fire hand) the tension will be the root cause of the actual creativity – the artistic outbursts will be volcanic channels for the pent up emotions engendered by the tensions represented by the Simian line. One cannot help noting that the Simian line is found on two entirely different classes of people – one class of a somewhat Earthy criminal type, and the other class of a deeply religious type. The factor in common between these different types is the inner tension which characterises their lives. One class is evolving as a result of the inner tension, whilst the other class is degenerating as a result of the same force. An important clue to the direction which the force will take is the finger patterns: as you might imagine, a series of pure whorls will surely indicate the evolving type, whilst the lower arches will indicate the involving types.

76 *A very strong Simian line running adross the palm.*

77 *A disruptive Simian line in which the two main lines are linked together by a strong subsidiary line. This formation is quite rare on an Air hand of this kind.*

77

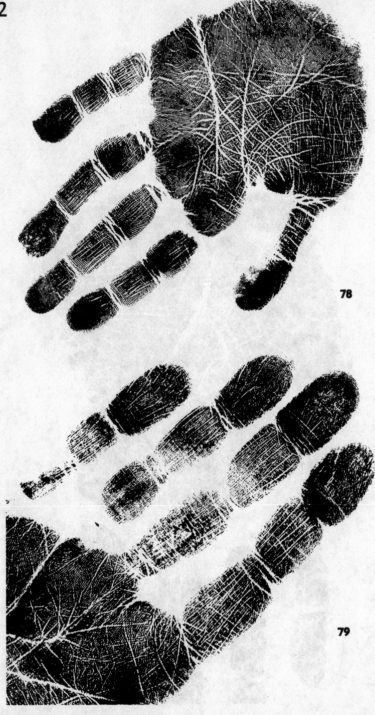

78

79

The Line of Life

THE length of the Lifeline will give a clue to the
quality of the subject's physical energy. I must re-
peat here that the length of the Lifeline has nothing
to do with the length of the subject's life, as so many
palmists would insist. The longer the line, and the
cleaner the quality of the line, the deeper the physical resources of the subject. The course of the Life
line demarcates the mount of Venus which, as we
have seen, is a reservoir of energies. The wider the
sweep of the line of Life the larger the reservoir,
and the greater the energy potential. With such a
line (plate 77), provided the quality of the line is
reasonable and clear, one can assume that the physical constitution of the subject is excellent.

Whatever the length and course of the line if it is
built up of a series of parallel lines of a weak nature
or if it is very badly chained (plate 78) we must
assume that the energy of the subject passes out very
unevenly. Rapid and purposeful activity alternates
fairly rapidly with inactive torpor.

When the line arises high in the hand, above the
line of Head, or even from the mount of Jupiter
(plate 82) there will be a strong ambitious motive to
all actions. Each move will be calculated. The passage of energies from an active zone of the hand pass
freely into the passive zone with distinctly Jupit-
erian characteristics as a result. The line or series
of lines which traverse the beginning of the Head
line and join the Life line to the mount of Jupiter
(plate 79) is even recognised by some palmists as a
separate line, and is called the line of Ambition. It is
a certain sign of an overdeveloped and highly
sensitive ego which can be easily hurt and damaged
when the ambitious dreams are impeded.

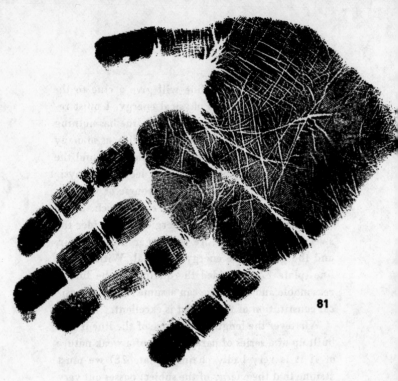

81

We have already discussed to some extent the significance of a strong joining of the line of Life to the line of Head. Shrewdness and a reluctance to make decisions is the chief characteristic represented.

Should the Life line spring unimpaired from above the thumb, completely unattached to the line of Head, we can assume that the 'controlling' influence of the head on actions is less marked: the subject will be impulsive in action.

A Life line which is deflected from the normal course and ends up on the mount of Moon (plate 80) indicates that the physical energies are unstable and badly directed.

78 *A weak line of Life on the hand of a young girl.*
79 *A line of Ambition.*
80 *A Life line verging towards the mount of Moon at its termination.*
81 *The fire hand of a young boy, with the Life line terminating on the mount of Moon.*

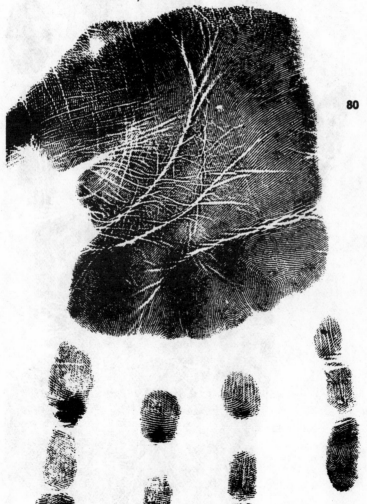

80

82 *Good lines of Apollo on the hand of
a television and radio actress.*
83 *A male Fire hand with several
strong lines in the Girdle, and a very
weak Fate line.*

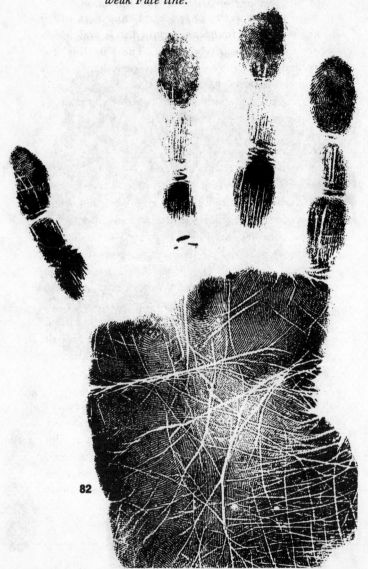

82

Subsidiary Lines

THE three main lines of Heart, Head and Life are very rarely absent on hands — sometimes the existence of a Simian line would suggest the absence of either Head or Heart, but once the nature of the Simian line is understood this error will be recognised. However, there are several other lines which are sometimes found on certain hands and which are sometimes entirely absent. The Fate line, for example, is absent on about one in five hands. Such lines are referred to as 'subsidiaries'. Their significance can best be understood by regarding them as conductors of energies, as with the main lines, but as one or two of these subsidary lines do conform to certain patterns we shall examine their characteristics here. The Girdle of Venus (see plate 73) may be regarded as a subsidiary line, as may the line of Ambition (plate 79). The remaining important lines are the lines of Fate, Mercury and Apollo.

All the other subsidiary lines are less important. They are usually hair lines conducting energies in certain directions. The mesh of vacillatory lines found on the characteristic Water hand indicate the variety of directions both emotional and mental which is typical of the type. The more pronounced lines running across the mount of Venus in the Earth hand at plate 87, for example, are fairly distinctive and manifest characteristics which are unique to a well known singer in a 'pop' group.

The line of Fate is related to the inner adaptability of the subject. As the line runs up the centre of the hand, it may be regarded as demarcating the conscious side of the hand from the unconscious, and, rather like the finger of Saturn, it may be considered as a sort of balance line between these

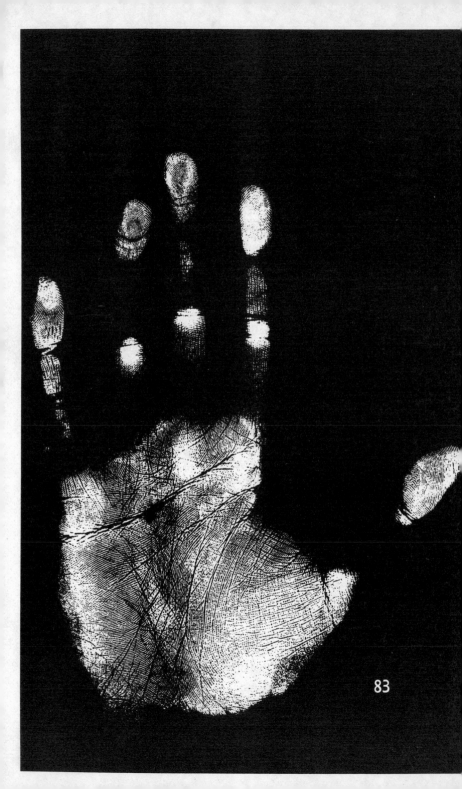

83

84 *The right hand print of the actress at plate 82, showing several lines of Apollo.*

85 *The hand of a World famous negro jazzman, with a Simian line, strong line of Heart, Fate and Life, an imaginative Head line and a well developed line of Apollo. There are rich whorls on each finger, and the hand is of a predominately Fire type, with Earth lines. A very rich personality type.*

84

two forces. The stronger this line is – the more perfectly formed, and the longer its course – the more adaptable the subject will be. Adaptability is essential to our lives where everything is changing all the time, and in general we can say that the more adaptable the subject, the more harmony and purposive direction he will find in himself. The purposive direction represented by a good line of Fate must be related to the hand type as a whole.

The line of Mercury conducts energies from the seat of the subconscious to the active world (plate 45). It is an indication of the degree to which the subject's intuition is developed. The line is found on such people as clairvoyants and highly intuitive types who have an emotional understanding of matters which supercedes the intellectual level of understanding. It is a line most often composed of several hair lines jerkily connected.

The line of Apollo is usually quite short (plate 82 is a good example of the line in its common form). The line is directly related to the creativity of the person.

Although the actual presence of the line cannot be taken as a sure sign of creativity it can be taken as an indication of the *wish* to create. Whether or not the urge is fulfilled will depend on other factors which can be determined from the hand. If, instead of one single line, there are numerous small lines making up the Apollo formation, you must interpret that many small talents are requiring fulfilment, and that these are very likely being only partially satisfied. The traditional interpretation of such lines is that the subject is a 'jack of all trades, master of none'.

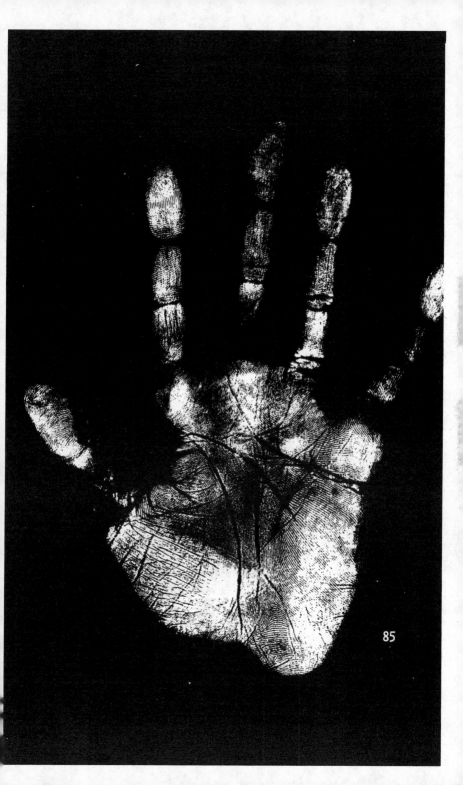

85

132

86 The hand of a Spaniard, with a
short finger of Jupiter, and several
other indications of an inferiority
complex.

Conclusions

As I pointed out in the introduction – the purpose of this book is to form a simple introduction to the stimulating study of one of the most ancient sciences in the world. In studying the above text, and in trying to relate what you learn to your own collection of hands, you are building a scaffolding from which you may construct your own system of interpretations of one of the most fascinating subjects in the world. With what you have learned from this book you should be able to take your study further – look at hands, collect prints, study other books on palmistry, talk to people about palmistry and strive always to remain in that state of mind which will reject nothing as unworthy of attention and study and yet will be prepared to reject everything – even your own established certainties – in order to make new discoveries.

THE END

BIBLIOGRAPHY
ALLEN, E. M.
A Manual of Cheirosophy.

Ward Lock Ltd. 1885

A scholarly introduction to the theories held by the best palmists towards the end of the last century, as a result of the earlier research work of D'Arpentigny and Desbarrolles.
BELL, Sir Charles
The Hand – its Mechanism and Vital Endowment as Evincing Design.

Bridgewater Series 1833

Contains much valuable material on the hand, though of a general medical nature.
BENHAM, W. G.
The Laws of Scientific Hand Reading.

Various publishers 1900

Reprints and second-hand copies of this excellent book are easy to come by. It is a book essential to the serious student, containing prints and photographs of many interesting hands. The section on chirognomy is more valuable than the section on cheiromancy, which appears to be based more on reasoning than on systematic observation.
CARUS, G. C.
Über Grund und Bedeutung der verschiedenen Formen der Hand in verschiedenen Personen.

1846

German text only, which formulates a strikingly original (for the time) classification of four hand types, and heralds a new medical interest in the relationship between the hand and temperament.
CHEIRO (pseudonym
for Count Louis Hamon)
Cheiro's Language of the Hand. 1894
Various publishers of the many editions. Second-hand copies are fairly easy to come by – the text is largely garbled and inaccurate, and it is extremely difficult to understand how Cheiro became so very famous as a palmist – he contributed nothing of value to the science and harmed much which might have been valuable. It remains, however, the kind of palmistry 'system' which is popular even today, and perhaps for this reason alone one should become familiar with what Cheiro has to say. The interest of the book lies in the numerous hands of well known people that are illustrated.

CUMMINS & MIDLO
Finger Prints, Palms and Soles.
Dover Publications 1961
A very detailed account of the study of skin patterns on the hands and feet, containing much peripheral material of interest to palmists.

D'ARPENTINGNY, C. S.
La Chirognomie, où l'art de reconnaitre les tendences de l'intelligence d'après les formes de la main.
1843
The classic book on chirognomy. This is esesntial to the student, for D'Arpentigny's classification of seven hand types has formed the basis of almost all palmistic systems up to the present time. It must not be forgotton that the classification is, by the best modern standards, out of date. There is an English translation 'The Science of the Hand' by E. M. Allen (1886), but this is not generally obtainable.

DESBARROLLES, A.
Les Mystères de la Main.
1859
The famous classic on cheiromancy. This was the first of several books on palmistry and although it is replete with occult and astrological references, and although it is not available in translation, the next is necessary reading for the keen student.

GETTINGS, F.
The Book of the Hand.
Paul Hamlyn 1965
A profusely illustrated account of handreading, with the first serious general history of palmistry.

JAQUIN, N.
The Signature of Time
Faber and Faber 1940
The Hand Speaks.
Lyndoe & Fisher 1942
The Human Hand — the Living Symbol.
Rockliff 1956
All these books make good background reading. The latter claims to be the result of forty years of research, experiment and study.

MANGOLDT, U. V.
La Main de Votre Enfant.
Neuchâtel – Paris, Delachaux & Niestlè 1957
The French translation of the German text, *Kinderhände Sprechen*. There is no English version available. The book contains many original observations and is not exclusively related to the hand of the child.

MUCHERY, G.
Traité Complet de la Chiromancie Déductive et Experimentale.
Editions Chariot 1958
Available only in French, the text makes some attempt to relate palmistry to astrology, and although the results are not entirely successful some of the underlying philosophy is of value. Several famous French hands are somewhat badly reproduced.

SABATTINI, G.
Bibliografia di Opere Antiche e Moderne di Chiromanzia.
Nironi and Prandi – Reggio Emilia 1946
The only good bibliography of palmistry – contains short biographies of leading authors and palmists.
This book is really of very great value to those palmists who are interested in the history of their subject.

SPIER, J.
The Hands of Children.
Routledge and Kegan Paul 1944
Translation from Germany by V. Grove. One of the best books on palmistry today – essential reading for the student. The second edition, which contains an interesting collection of prints and an appendix on the hands of the mentally diseased by Levi, is the copy to acquire, for this contains a series of analyses of interesting hands.

VASCHIDE, N.
Essai sur la Psychologie de la Main.
1909
Published posthumously by the author's wife. Based on Vaschide's own experimental findings – his premature death prevented his ideas from being completely assimilated and worked out. Excellent reading, both from a historical and practical standpoint.

ERIC BURDON – Vocalist in "The Animals".

THE heavy square palm, the short thick fingers, and
the heavy papillary ridges indicate that he is basically of the Earth type. This means that he is essentially an extroverted personality, who will find
pleasure in rhythmic movements, and who attempts
to express himself in a physical way. An Earth hand
is usually a little more simple in some ways than
Eric's, and although we see the loop-like patterns on
the finger tips which indicate a basic gentleness of
character, the presence of numerous lines indicate
that he will be a little erratic in behaviour. The
complex series of lines which run across the palm
from the base of the thumb towards the gap between
the little finger and the ring finger is evidence that
the essential gentleness is punctuated by periods in
which Eric is forced into a restless search for self-
expression. These lines are, in this particular hand
formation, almost a destructive element, combining
three phases of an energy lacking in controlled
direction.

The first phase – that represented by the lines
which cut across the ball of the thumb – indicates
that energy of a strong emotional kind (so strong as
to demand immediate release) is forcing itself out.
This energy is channeled into two lines which join
the line of Head to the line of Heart, a formation
which is usually called a 'simian line' and which is
a sure indication of energies contained under pressure. A simian line in this type of hand may be regarded as a mark of the sort of inner tension directly
related to the creative act. The third phase of energy
is represented by the lines which disappear into the
gap between the ring finger and the little finger:
these lines in traditional palmistry are regarded as

lines of creativity. The fact that the last phase of this strong energy is so weak and broken suggests a deal of uncertainty in Eric about his art form – he is probably more interested in the actual making of the music than in the effect it has on his audience. We see that the lines are displaced towards the little finger, and that in fact all the lines we have just studied verge towards the little fingers – this means that the final artistic form will contain a strong sexual element.

Fortunately for Eric, the line of Heart comes well into the space between the first finger and the middle finger, indicating a healthy sexual balance, and we can deduce that although the original force of energy has to be expressed in a physical and creative way, with a considerable exhaustion of creative sexual power, Eric can nonetheless separate these energies (which are so strong as to render him merely an instrument in their power) from his own private life. As a representative of the complex Earth type, Eric's hand is particularly interesting – a likeable personality with a strong creative direction. The hands of the other *Animals* I examined had similar strong Earth tendencies. It is amusing that a Victorian writer on palmistry should describe a similar type of hand as 'animal-like'!

87 The hand of Eric Burdon.

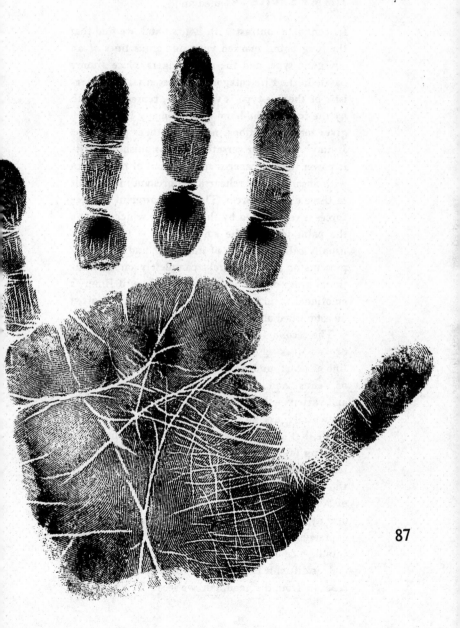

87

JIMMY SAVILE – Comedian

In complete contrast with Eric's hand, we find that
the long palm, marked with numerous lines of an
energetic type, and the short fingers, place Jimmy
Savile in the Fire category. The essential characteristic of the fire type is versatility, represented both
by the form of the hand and the many lines, which
gives many directions, not all of them productive.
Jimmy's particular versatility and astonishing artistic power (he can caper madly in front of the camera
with absolutely no rehearsal beforehand) is a result
of three distinct forces. The most powerful of these
forces is represented by the long line which runs up
the palm towards the small finger – this line is
usually called the 'line of intuition', and it here represents an ability to rely completely on an emotional grasp of a situation. So quickly will Jimmy's
emotional faculties work that he himself will often
be astonished at what he says and does.

The second force is represented by the series of
broken lines which runs above and parallel to the
line of heart, under the finger roots, called a 'girdle
of Venus', and indicates a need for constant change
and variety – this in a fire type who is already fun-
damentally unstable in normal social terms. The
single, but strong, line of creativity dropping from
the ring finger redeems to some extent this state of
inner restlessness, and gives a creative direction to
the intuitive forces. Just as Eric is almost a 'victim'
of a need for constant physical expression, so is
Jimmy a victim of a need for a constant emotional
expression. From the line of Head we see a strong
intelligence and a surprising degree of practicality.

It is difficult for us to imagine Jimmy as a person
separate from the 'madman' we see on T. V., but like

all good Fire types he is essentially extroverted yet always aware of a certain insecurity himself. A good creative Fire type often secretly thinks of himself as a confidence trickster, and this is almost a complete statement of Jimmy's position, for he is are that his talent, his capering and frolicking on the verge of exhibitionism, is almost a result of what might be called 'artistic drunkeness', and his normal life, though lived under strong pressures, is surprisingly sober in its lack of direction. In Eric's hand we saw that creativity sprang from a strong physical urge which sought expression in rhythm — but in Jimmy's hand we see that the creativity springs from his inner emotional restlessness and is given form by his unique intuitive faculty.

88 *The hand of Jimmy Savile.*

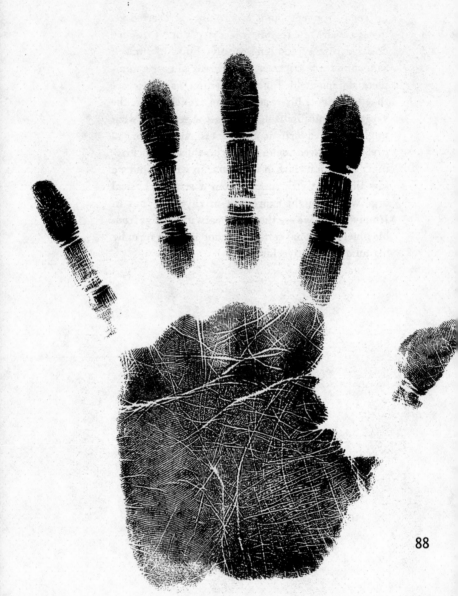

88

KEITH FORDYCE – announcer and compère.

THE square palm and long flexible fingers of Keith
Fordyce's hand indicates that he is essentially an Air
type, with the sort of personality which can best be
given fulfilment by establishing relationships with
things and people. Two important factors in the
hand indicate that Keith is a very special personality – the series of almost concentric whorl patterns
on the finger tips is quite a rare phenomenon, and
indicates a fairly highly - strung individuality. The
patterns are more commonly found on Fire hands
and accompany a talented restlessness more common to this type.

Another name for the Air type is 'Intellectual hand',
indicative of Keith's clear mentality and quick pro-
bing intellect – note the downward curve of the head
line which lends imaginative elements to a type essentially sympathetic by nature. It is these characteristics which, taken in regard to the basic need to
relate himself to people and things (the ideal quality
in a commentator, one would think) account for his
success. The second rare phenomenon in Keith's
hand is the fewness of the lines. This is most unex-
pected in an Air hand, and since it is more a strong
characteristic of the Earth type, we must expect
certain Earth qualities behind the structure of
Keith's personality – a reliability and an element of
directness, and perhaps also an element of suspicion
which, in an Air hand, will manifest itself in the
form of sympathetic questioning.

*89 The hand of Keith Fordyce. The
palm is in fact square, though in the
print it tends to look longish.*
90 The hand of Alma Cogan.

ALMA COGAN – Popular singer

THE long narrow palm and long fingers of Alma Cogan's hand indicate that she is essentially a Water type. Although the palm of this type in its pure form is covered with a mesh of lines, the lively quality of Alma's lines indicates that she has strong Fire tendencies. In short this means that Alma is caught between two strong forces – one watery force which requires stability and security, and a fire force which 'boils' the water and creates strong inner tensions. Alma's life is given its creative form in several ways, but the rare quality in the hand is the long line of head with a marked upward turn at the end. This indicates a sort of practicality which is usually absent in a Water type – the most unpractical of the four types. It is this practicality, and the strong lines of ambition which run up from the top of the life line towards the first finger, which lends Alma the ability to deal with the difficult world of show business. The strong ambition is given a distinct creative turn by the presence of a whorl pattern on the first finger, which is sometimes referred to in traditional palmistry as the finger of ambition.

Like Jimmy Savile, Alma has a marked Girdle of Venus, which in part explains the restlessness of her personality and her love of travel. Alma has a long line of intuition which is so necessary to one in her profession, but the fact that it is so broken indicates a feeling of insecurity, proper to her type, which her sense of practical requirements and her ambition are constantly fighting. Alma's hand is remarkable for its strong contradictory forces – in outward life there is a positive direction, but inwardly this is paralleled with a lack of direction and uncertainty.

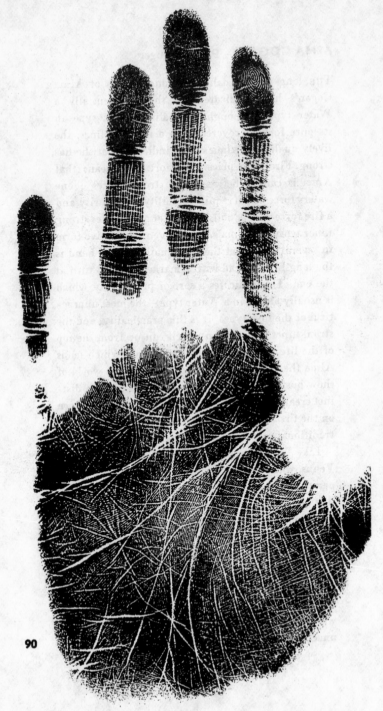

90

91

QUESTIONS

On page 148 to 155 there are hand prints. Look at these carefully, and then attempt to answer these questions. The answers will be found by referring to page 156.

1. Four of the prints are males—which are they?
2. Of the five female prints, three are Water hands, which are they?
3. One print is of a highly extraverted and gifted artist—which is it?
4. Two of these prints belong to identical twins—which are they?
5. One of the girls in this collection is the sister of the young man at plate 93—which is she? It is possible to identify her by the finger patterns.
6. Can you determine the predominant types of each hand?
7. One of the girls has a strong urge to take drugs—which would you say she is?
8. Which of the prints reveals a deeply imaginative personality.
9. Several of the hands indicate strong intuitive abilities, but which of the persons represented here will be able to make practical use of their strong intutions?

91 The hand of an artist.
92 The hand of a typist.

92

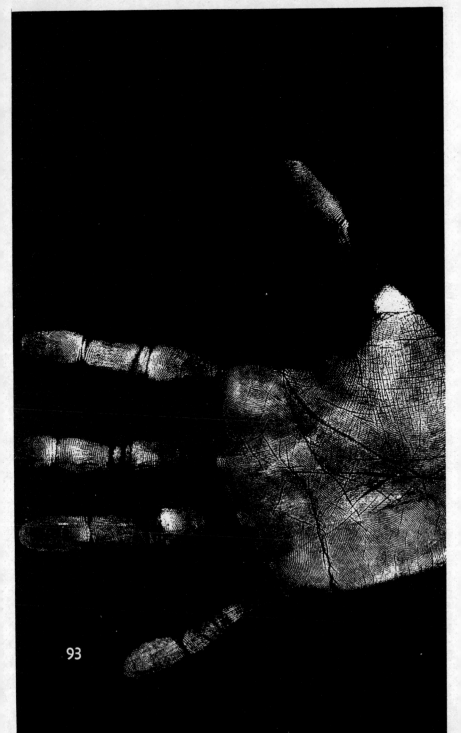

93

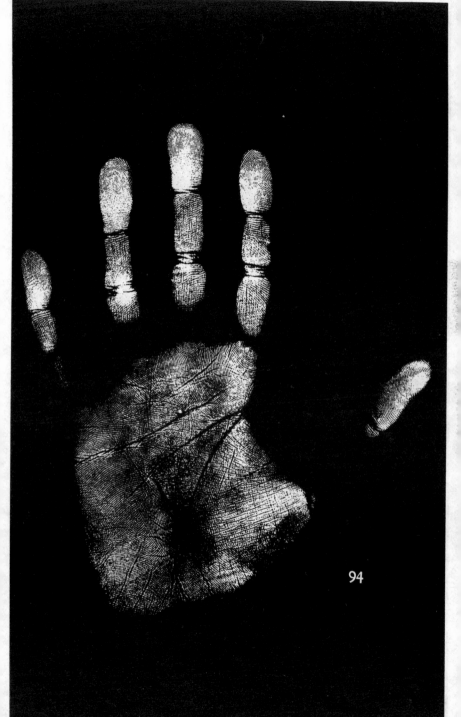

94

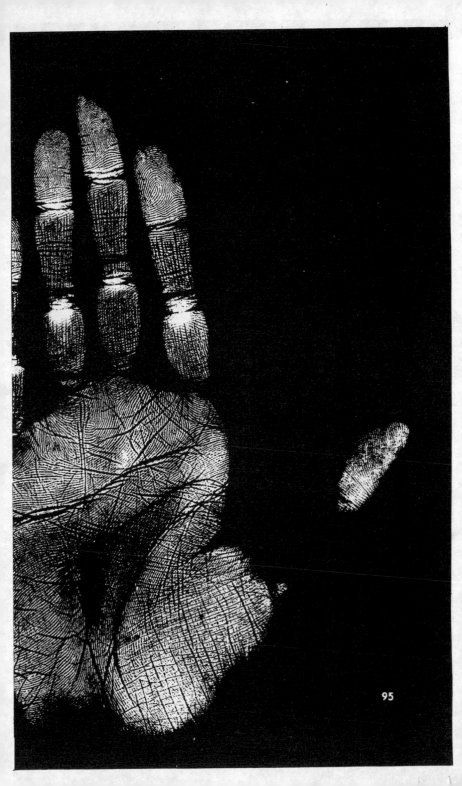

95

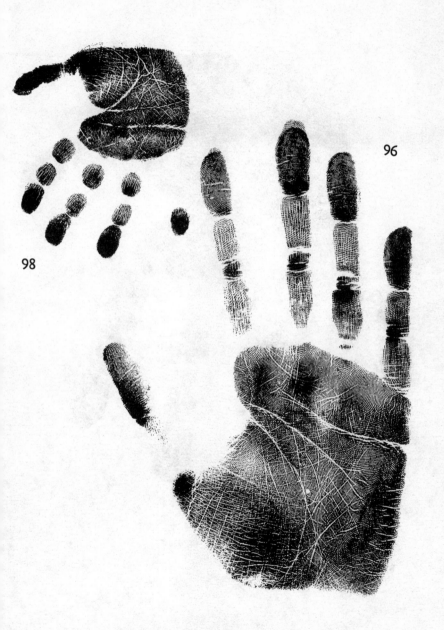

96

98

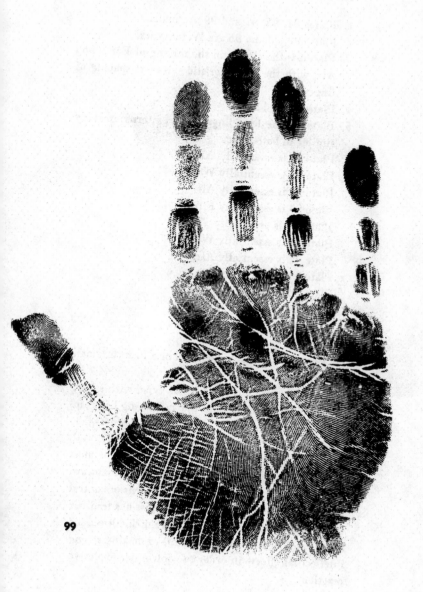

99

ANSWERS

1. Plates 91, 93, 97 and 99 are male.
2. Plates 92, 95 and 96 are Water types.
3. Plate 91—the clue is in the mixing of Earth and Air, with the characteristic extravert spacing of fingers.
4. Plates 92 and 95.
5. Plate 96—the long finger loop patterns are very similar in both hands.
6. Plate 91 is essentially Air.
   Plate 92 is essentially Water.
   Plate 93 is essentially Air.
   Plate 94 is essentially Fire.
   Plate 95 is essentially Water.
   Plate 96 is essentially Water.
   Plate 97 is essentially Air.
   Plate 98 is essentially Air.
   Plate 99 is essentially Fire.
7. Plate 94.
8. Plate 91.
9. Plate 91.

See Plate 42, page 75 — the hand of a French female psychologist.

The hand is basically of the Fire type, with a long palm and short fingers, but the vacillating lines and their chained condition suggests a strong Water tendency also. Water and Fire do not mix very well, so the temperament will be fairly explosive — almost always on the point of "boiling over". The upward turn of the head line indicates an element of control and as the training of this psychologist has lead her to see something of her emotional difficulties, she has learned to appreciate the value of making strong intellectual efforts in order to control her explosive reactions.

MELVIN POWERS SELF-IMPROVEMENT LIBRARY

ASTROLOGY
_____ASTROLOGY: HOW TO CHART YOUR HOROSCOPE *Max Heindel* 3.00
_____ASTROLOGY: YOUR PERSONAL SUN-SIGN GUIDE *Beatrice Ryder* 3.00
_____ASTROLOGY FOR EVERYDAY LIVING *Janet Harris* 2.00
_____ASTROLOGY MADE EASY *Astarte* 3.00
_____ASTROLOGY MADE PRACTICAL *Alexandra Kayhle* 3.00
_____ASTROLOGY, ROMANCE, YOU AND THE STARS *Anthony Norvell* 4.00
_____MY WORLD OF ASTROLOGY *Sydney Omarr* 5.00
_____THOUGHT DIAL *Sydney Omarr* 4.00
_____WHAT THE STARS REVEAL ABOUT THE MEN IN YOUR LIFE *Thelma White* 3.00

BRIDGE
_____BRIDGE BIDDING MADE EASY *Edwin B. Kantar* 5.00
_____BRIDGE CONVENTIONS *Edwin B. Kantar* 5.00
_____BRIDGE HUMOR *Edwin B. Kantar* 3.00
_____COMPETITIVE BIDDING IN MODERN BRIDGE *Edgar Kaplan* 4.00
_____DEFENSIVE BRIDGE PLAY COMPLETE *Edwin B. Kantar* 10.00
_____HOW TO IMPROVE YOUR BRIDGE *Alfred Sheinwold* 3.00
_____IMPROVING YOUR BIDDING SKILLS *Edwin B. Kantar* 4.00
_____INTRODUCTION TO DEFENDER'S PLAY *Edwin B. Kantar* 3.00
_____SHORT CUT TO WINNING BRIDGE *Alfred Sheinwold* 3.00
_____TEST YOUR BRIDGE PLAY *Edwin B. Kantar* 3.00
_____WINNING DECLARER PLAY *Dorothy Hayden Truscott* 4.00

BUSINESS, STUDY & REFERENCE
_____CONVERSATION MADE EASY *Elliot Russell* 2.00
_____EXAM SECRET *Dennis B. Jackson* 3.00
_____FIX-IT BOOK *Arthur Symons* 2.00
_____HOW TO DEVELOP A BETTER SPEAKING VOICE *M. Hellier* 3.00
_____HOW TO MAKE A FORTUNE IN REAL ESTATE *Albert Winnikoff* 4.00
_____INCREASE YOUR LEARNING POWER *Geoffrey A. Dudley* 2.00
_____MAGIC OF NUMBERS *Robert Tocquet* 2.00
_____PRACTICAL GUIDE TO BETTER CONCENTRATION *Melvin Powers* 3.00
_____PRACTICAL GUIDE TO PUBLIC SPEAKING *Maurice Forley* 3.00
_____7 DAYS TO FASTER READING *William S. Schaill* 3.00
_____SONGWRITERS RHYMING DICTIONARY *Jane Shaw Whitfield* 5.00
_____SPELLING MADE EASY *Lester D. Basch & Dr. Milton Finkelstein* 2.00
_____STUDENT'S GUIDE TO BETTER GRADES *J. A. Rickard* 3.00
_____TEST YOURSELF—Find Your Hidden Talent *Jack Shafer* 3.00
_____YOUR WILL & WHAT TO DO ABOUT IT *Attorney Samuel G. Kling* 3.00

CALLIGRAPHY
_____ADVANCED CALLIGRAPHY *Katherine Jeffares* 7.00
_____CALLIGRAPHER'S REFERENCE BOOK *Anne Leptich & Jacque Evans* 6.00
_____CALLIGRAPHY—The Art of Beautiful Writing *Katherine Jeffares* 7.00
_____CALLIGRAPHY FOR FUN & PROFIT *Anne Leptich & Jacque Evans* 7.00
_____CALLIGRAPHY MADE EASY *Tina Serafini* 7.00

CHESS & CHECKERS
_____BEGINNER'S GUIDE TO WINNING CHESS *Fred Reinfeld* 3.00
_____BETTER CHESS—How to Play *Fred Reinfeld* 2.00
_____CHECKERS MADE EASY *Tom Wiswell* 2.00
_____CHESS IN TEN EASY LESSONS *Larry Evans* 3.00
_____CHESS MADE EASY *Milton L. Hanauer* 3.00
_____CHESS PROBLEMS FOR BEGINNERS *edited by Fred Reinfeld* 2.00
_____CHESS SECRETS REVEALED *Fred Reinfeld* 2.00
_____CHESS STRATEGY—An Expert's Guide *Fred Reinfeld* 2.00
_____CHESS TACTICS FOR BEGINNERS *edited by Fred Reinfeld* 3.00
_____CHESS THEORY & PRACTICE *Morry & Mitchell* 2.00
_____HOW TO WIN AT CHECKERS *Fred Reinfeld* 3.00
_____1001 BRILLIANT WAYS TO CHECKMATE *Fred Reinfeld* 4.00
_____1001 WINNING CHESS SACRIFICES & COMBINATIONS *Fred Reinfeld* 4.00
_____SOVIET CHESS *Edited by R. G. Wade* 3.00

COOKERY & HERBS

____CULPEPER'S HERBAL REMEDIES *Dr. Nicholas Culpeper*	3.00
____FAST GOURMET COOKBOOK *Poppy Cannon*	2.50
____GINSENG The Myth & The Truth *Joseph P. Hou*	3.00
____HEALING POWER OF HERBS *May Bethel*	3.00
____HEALING POWER OF NATURAL FOODS *May Bethel*	3.00
____HERB HANDBOOK *Dawn MacLeod*	3.00
____HERBS FOR COOKING AND HEALING *Dr. Donald Law*	2.00
____HERBS FOR HEALTH—How to Grow & Use Them *Louise Evans Doole*	3.00
____HOME GARDEN COOKBOOK—Delicious Natural Food Recipes *Ken Kraft*	3.00
____MEDICAL HERBALIST *edited by Dr. J. R. Yemm*	3.00
____NATURAL FOOD COOKBOOK *Dr. Harry C. Bond*	3.00
____NATURE'S MEDICINES *Richard Lucas*	3.00
____VEGETABLE GARDENING FOR BEGINNERS *Hugh Wiberg*	2.00
____VEGETABLES FOR TODAY'S GARDENS *R. Milton Carleton*	2.00
____VEGETARIAN COOKERY *Janet Walker*	4.00
____VEGETARIAN COOKING MADE EASY & DELECTABLE *Veronica Vezza*	3.00
____VEGETARIAN DELIGHTS—A Happy Cookbook for Health *K. R. Mehta*	2.00
____VEGETARIAN GOURMET COOKBOOK *Joyce McKinnel*	3.00

GAMBLING & POKER

____ADVANCED POKER STRATEGY & WINNING PLAY *A. D. Livingston*	3.00
____HOW NOT TO LOSE AT POKER *Jeffrey Lloyd Castle*	3.00
____HOW TO WIN AT DICE GAMES *Skip Frey*	3.00
____HOW TO WIN AT POKER *Terence Reese & Anthony T. Watkins*	3.00
____SECRETS OF WINNING POKER *George S. Coffin*	3.00
____WINNING AT CRAPS *Dr. Lloyd T. Commins*	3.00
____WINNING AT GIN *Chester Wander & Cy Rice*	3.00
____WINNING AT POKER—An Expert's Guide *John Archer*	3.00
____WINNING AT 21—An Expert's Guide *John Archer*	4.00
____WINNING POKER SYSTEMS *Norman Zadeh*	3.00

HEALTH

____BEE POLLEN *Lynda Lyngheim & Jack Scagnetti*	3.00
____DR. LINDNER'S SPECIAL WEIGHT CONTROL METHOD *P. G. Lindner, M.D.*	1.50
____HELP YOURSELF TO BETTER SIGHT *Margaret Darst Corbett*	3.00
____HOW TO IMPROVE YOUR VISION *Dr. Robert A. Kraskin*	3.00
____HOW YOU CAN STOP SMOKING PERMANENTLY *Ernest Caldwell*	3.00
____MIND OVER PLATTER *Peter G. Lindner, M.D.*	3.00
____NATURE'S WAY TO NUTRITION & VIBRANT HEALTH *Robert J. Scrutton*	3.00
____NEW CARBOHYDRATE DIET COUNTER *Patti Lopez-Pereira*	1.50
____QUICK & EASY EXERCISES FOR FACIAL BEAUTY *Judy Smith-deal*	2.00
____QUICK & EASY EXERCISES FOR FIGURE BEAUTY *Judy Smith-deal*	2.00
____REFLEXOLOGY *Dr. Maybelle Segal*	3.00
____REFLEXOLOGY FOR GOOD HEALTH *Anna Kaye & Don C. Matchan*	3.00
____YOU CAN LEARN TO RELAX *Dr. Samuel Gutwirth*	3.00
____YOUR ALLERGY—What To Do About It *Allan Knight, M.D.*	3.00

HOBBIES

____BEACHCOMBING FOR BEGINNERS *Norman Hickin*	2.00
____BLACKSTONE'S MODERN CARD TRICKS *Harry Blackstone*	3.00
____BLACKSTONE'S SECRETS OF MAGIC *Harry Blackstone*	3.00
____COIN COLLECTING FOR BEGINNERS *Burton Hobson & Fred Reinfeld*	3.00
____ENTERTAINING WITH ESP *Tony 'Doc' Shiels*	2.00
____400 FASCINATING MAGIC TRICKS YOU CAN DO *Howard Thurston*	3.00
____HOW I TURN JUNK INTO FUN AND PROFIT *Sari*	3.00
____HOW TO WRITE A HIT SONG & SELL IT *Tommy Boyce*	7.00
____JUGGLING MADE EASY *Rudolf Dittrich*	2.00
____MAGIC MADE EASY *Byron Wels*	2.00
____STAMP COLLECTING FOR BEGINNERS *Burton Hobson*	2.00

HYPNOTISM

____ADVANCED TECHNIQUES OF HYPNOSIS *Melvin Powers*	2.00

BRAINWASHING AND THE CULTS *Paul A. Verdier, Ph.D.* 3.00
CHILDBIRTH WITH HYPNOSIS *William S. Kroger, M.D.* 3.00
HOW TO SOLVE Your Sex Problems with Self-Hypnosis *Frank S. Caprio, M.D.* 3.00
HOW TO STOP SMOKING THRU SELF-HYPNOSIS *Leslie M. LeCron* 3.00
HOW TO USE AUTO-SUGGESTION EFFECTIVELY *John Duckworth* 3.00
HOW YOU CAN BOWL BETTER USING SELF-HYPNOSIS *Jack Heise* 3.00
HOW YOU CAN PLAY BETTER GOLF USING SELF-HYPNOSIS *Jack Heise* 3.00
HYPNOSIS AND SELF-HYPNOSIS *Bernard Hollander, M.D.* 3.00
HYPNOTISM *(Originally published in 1893) Carl Sextus* 5.00
HYPNOTISM & PSYCHIC PHENOMENA *Simeon Edmunds* 4.00
HYPNOTISM MADE EASY *Dr. Ralph Winn* 3.00
HYPNOTISM MADE PRACTICAL *Louis Orton* 3.00
HYPNOTISM REVEALED *Melvin Powers* 2.00
HYPNOTISM TODAY *Leslie LeCron and Jean Bordeaux, Ph.D.* 5.00
MODERN HYPNOSIS *Lesley Kuhn & Salvatore Russo, Ph.D.* 5.00
NEW CONCEPTS OF HYPNOSIS *Bernard C. Gindes, M.D.* 5.00
NEW SELF-HYPNOSIS *Paul Adams* 4.00
POST-HYPNOTIC INSTRUCTIONS—Suggestions for Therapy *Arnold Furst* 3.00
PRACTICAL GUIDE TO SELF-HYPNOSIS *Melvin Powers* 3.00
PRACTICAL HYPNOTISM *Philip Magonet, M.D.* 3.00
SECRETS OF HYPNOTISM *S. J. Van Pelt, M.D.* 3.00
SELF-HYPNOSIS A Conditioned-Response Technique *Laurance Sparks* 5.00
SELF-HYPNOSIS Its Theory, Technique & Application *Melvin Powers* 3.00
THERAPY THROUGH HYPNOSIS edited by *Raphael H. Rhodes* 4.00

JUST FOR WOMEN
COSMOPOLITAN'S GUIDE TO MARVELOUS MEN Fwd. by *Helen Gurley Brown* 3.00
COSMOPOLITAN'S HANG-UP HANDBOOK Foreword by *Helen Gurley Brown* 4.00
COSMOPOLITAN'S LOVE BOOK—A Guide to Ecstasy in Bed 4.00
COSMOPOLITAN'S NEW ETIQUETTE GUIDE Fwd. by *Helen Gurley Brown* 4.00
I AM A COMPLEAT WOMAN *Doris Hagopian & Karen O'Connor Sweeney* 3.00
JUST FOR WOMEN—A Guide to the Female Body *Richard E. Sand, M.D.* 4.00
NEW APPROACHES TO SEX IN MARRIAGE *John E. Eichenlaub, M.D.* 3.00
SEXUALLY ADEQUATE FEMALE *Frank S. Caprio, M.D.* 3.00
YOUR FIRST YEAR OF MARRIAGE *Dr. Tom McGinnis* 3.00

MARRIAGE, SEX & PARENTHOOD
ABILITY TO LOVE *Dr. Allan Fromme* 5.00
ENCYCLOPEDIA OF MODERN SEX & LOVE TECHNIQUES *Macandrew* 5.00
GUIDE TO SUCCESSFUL MARRIAGE *Drs. Albert Ellis & Robert Harper* 5.00
HOW TO RAISE AN EMOTIONALLY HEALTHY, HAPPY CHILD *A. Ellis* 3.00
IMPOTENCE & FRIGIDITY *Edwin W. Hirsch, M.D.* 3.00
SEX WITHOUT GUILT *Albert Ellis, Ph.D.* 3.00
SEXUALLY ADEQUATE MALE *Frank S. Caprio, M.D.* 3.00

METAPHYSICS & OCCULT
BOOK OF TALISMANS, AMULETS & ZODIACAL GEMS *William Pavitt* 4.00
CONCENTRATION—A Guide to Mental Mastery *Mouni Sadhu* 3.00
CRITIQUES OF GOD Edited by *Peter Angeles* 7.00
DREAMS & OMENS REVEALED *Fred Gettings* 3.00
EXTRA-TERRESTRIAL INTELLIGENCE—The First Encounter 6.00
FORTUNE TELLING WITH CARDS *P. Foli* 3.00
HANDWRITING ANALYSIS MADE EASY *John Marley* 3.00
HANDWRITING TELLS *Nadya Olyanova* 5.00
HOW TO UNDERSTAND YOUR DREAMS *Geoffrey A. Dudley* 3.00
ILLUSTRATED YOGA *William Zorn* 3.00
IN DAYS OF GREAT PEACE *Mouni Sadhu* 3.00
KING SOLOMON'S TEMPLE IN THE MASONIC TRADITION *Alex Horne* 5.00
LSD—THE AGE OF MIND *Bernard Roseman* 2.00
MAGICIAN—His training and work *W. E. Butler* 3.00
MEDITATION *Mouni Sadhu* 5.00
MODERN NUMEROLOGY *Morris C. Goodman* 3.00
NUMEROLOGY—ITS FACTS AND SECRETS *Ariel Yvon Taylor* 3.00

_____NUMEROLOGY MADE EASY *W. Mykian* — 3.00
_____PALMISTRY MADE EASY *Fred Gettings* — 3.00
_____PALMISTRY MADE PRACTICAL *Elizabeth Daniels Squire* — 3.00
_____PALMISTRY SECRETS REVEALED *Henry Frith* — 3.00
_____PROPHECY IN OUR TIME *Martin Ebon* — 2.50
_____PSYCHOLOGY OF HANDWRITING *Nadya Olyanova* — 3.00
_____SUPERSTITION—Are you superstitious? *Eric Maple* — 2.00
_____TAROT *Mouni Sadhu* — 6.00
_____TAROT OF THE BOHEMIANS *Papus* — 5.00
_____WAYS TO SELF-REALIZATION *Mouni Sadhu* — 3.00
_____WHAT YOUR HANDWRITING REVEALS *Albert E. Hughes* — 2.00
_____WITCHCRAFT, MAGIC & OCCULTISM—A Fascinating History *W. B. Crow* — 5.00
_____WITCHCRAFT—THE SIXTH SENSE *Justine Glass* — 4.00
_____WORLD OF PSYCHIC RESEARCH *Hereward Carrington* — 2.00

SELF-HELP & INSPIRATIONAL

_____DAILY POWER FOR JOYFUL LIVING *Dr. Donald Curtis* — 3.00
_____DYNAMIC THINKING *Melvin Powers* — 2.00
_____EXUBERANCE—Your Guide to Happiness & Fulfillment *Dr. Paul Kurtz* — 3.00
_____GREATEST POWER IN THE UNIVERSE *U. S. Andersen* — 5.00
_____GROW RICH WHILE YOU SLEEP *Ben Sweetland* — 3.00
_____GROWTH THROUGH REASON *Albert Ellis, Ph.D.* — 4.00
_____GUIDE TO DEVELOPING YOUR POTENTIAL *Herbert A. Otto, Ph.D.* — 3.00
_____GUIDE TO LIVING IN BALANCE *Frank S. Caprio, M.D.* — 2.00
_____HELPING YOURSELF WITH APPLIED PSYCHOLOGY *R. Henderson* — 2.00
_____HELPING YOURSELF WITH PSYCHIATRY *Frank S. Caprio, M.D.* — 2.00
_____HOW TO ATTRACT GOOD LUCK *A. H. Z. Carr* — 4.00
_____HOW TO CONTROL YOUR DESTINY *Norvell* — 3.00
_____HOW TO DEVELOP A WINNING PERSONALITY *Martin Panzer* — 3.00
_____HOW TO DEVELOP AN EXCEPTIONAL MEMORY *Young & Gibson* — 4.00
_____HOW TO OVERCOME YOUR FEARS *M. P. Leahy, M.D.* — 3.00
_____HOW YOU CAN HAVE CONFIDENCE AND POWER *Les Giblin* — 3.00
_____HUMAN PROBLEMS & HOW TO SOLVE THEM *Dr. Donald Curtis* — 3.00
_____I CAN *Ben Sweetland* — 4.00
_____I WILL *Ben Sweetland* — 3.00
_____LEFT-HANDED PEOPLE *Michael Barsley* — 4.00
_____MAGIC IN YOUR MIND *U. S. Andersen* — 5.00
_____MAGIC OF THINKING BIG *Dr. David J. Schwartz* — 3.00
_____MAGIC POWER OF YOUR MIND *Walter M. Germain* — 4.00
_____MENTAL POWER THROUGH SLEEP SUGGESTION *Melvin Powers* — 3.00
_____NEW GUIDE TO RATIONAL LIVING *Albert Ellis, Ph.D. & R. Harper, Ph.D.* — 3.00
_____OUR TROUBLED SELVES *Dr. Allan Fromme* — 3.00
_____PSYCHO-CYBERNETICS *Maxwell Maltz, M.D.* — 2.00
_____SCIENCE OF MIND IN DAILY LIVING *Dr. Donald Curtis* — 3.00
_____SECRET OF SECRETS *U. S. Andersen* — 4.00
_____SECRET POWER OF THE PYRAMIDS *U. S. Andersen* — 5.00
_____STUTTERING AND WHAT YOU CAN DO ABOUT IT *W. Johnson, Ph.D.* — 2.50
_____SUCCESS-CYBERNETICS *U. S. Andersen* — 4.00
_____10 DAYS TO A GREAT NEW LIFE *William E. Edwards* — 3.00
_____THINK AND GROW RICH *Napoleon Hill* — 3.00
_____THREE MAGIC WORDS *U. S. Andersen* — 5.00
_____TREASURY OF COMFORT *edited by Rabbi Sidney Greenberg* — 5.00
_____TREASURY OF THE ART OF LIVING *Sidney S. Greenberg* — 5.00
_____YOU ARE NOT THE TARGET *Laura Huxley* — 4.00
_____YOUR SUBCONSCIOUS POWER *Charles M. Simmons* — 4.00
_____YOUR THOUGHTS CAN CHANGE YOUR LIFE *Dr. Donald Curtis* — 4.00

The books listed above can be obtained from your book dealer or directly from Melvin Powers. When ordering, please remit 50¢ per book postage & handling. Send for our free illustrated catalog of self-improvement books.

Melvin Powers
12015 Sherman Road, No. Hollywood, California 91605